Make Your *Connections* Count

Networking Know-How to Make Your Business Thrive

D1418044

THRIVE
PUBLISHING™

THRIVE Publishing
A Division of PowerDynamics Publishing, Inc.
San Francisco, California
www.thrivebooks.com

ISBN: 978-0-9829419-4-2

Library of Congress Control Number: 2011927277

Printed in the United States of America on acid-free paper.

URL Disclaimer
All Internet addresses provided in this book were valid at press time.
However, due to the dynamic nature of the Internet, some addresses
may have changed or sites may have changed or ceased to exist since
publication. While the co-authors and publisher regret any
inconvenience this may cause readers, no responsibility for any
such changes can be accepted by either the co-authors or the publisher.

We dedicate this book to you:

the professional who realizes the power of networking
in achieving your goals and in building a successful business;
the individual who wants to *make your connections count.*
We salute you for embracing more knowledge and
we celebrate your commitment to being a savvy networker.

The Co-Authors of *Make Your Connections Count*

Table of Contents

Acknowledgements

Expressing appreciation is a key part of making your connections count. Before we share our wisdom and experience with you, we have a few people to thank for turning our vision for this book into a reality.

This book is the brilliant concept of Caterina Rando, the founder of THRIVE Publishing™ and a respected business strategist and coach, with whom many of us have worked to grow our businesses. Working closely with many life coaches, consultants and other professionals, she realized how valuable the knowledge they possessed would be to those people wanting to truly make their connections count in their businesses. The result was putting our ideas into a comprehensive book on networking know-how.

Without Caterina's "take action" spirit, her positive attitude and her commitment to excellence, you would not be reading this book of which we are all so proud. She was supported by a dedicated team who worked diligently to put together the best possible book for you. We are truly grateful for everyone's stellar contribution.

To Ruth Schwartz, with her many years of experience and wisdom, who served as an ongoing guide throughout the project, your leadership of our production team was invaluable, and your support to all of the co-authors is deeply appreciated.

To Karen Gargiulo, who served as the project manager and copy editor for this book, we appreciate your patient guidance, thoughtful advice and genuine enthusiasm for our work, and we are truly grateful.

To Tammy Tribble and Tricia Principe, our designers extraordinaire, who brought their creative talents to the cover and book layout, thank you both for your enthusiasm, problem-solving and attention to detail throughout this project.

To LynAnn King and Laura Piester, who were instrumental in identifying each of us as an expert in our respective fields, we thank you for being such great matchmakers.

To Tony Lloyd and Rua Necaise, who provided us with their keen eyes and made sure we dotted all the i's and crossed all the t's, thank you for your support and contribution and for making us read so perfectly on paper.

The Co-Authors of *Making Your Connections Count*

Introduction

Congratulations! You have opened an incredible resource, packed with great ideas that can turn your networking efforts into a business-building machine. You are about to discover how to *make your connections count.*

Networking is much more than handing out business cards. It is about effective communication, sincere giving and consistent follow-through. It is about building relationships by actively seeking ways to help others while communicating your value.

With this book, you can quickly rev up your networking know-how. As top experts in each of our respective specialties, we've joined together to give you proven, highly effective networking strategies. Some bits of advice are repeated in different chapters—that should tell you how important that advice is!

It's all here—how-to's for social networking, event networking, giving great referrals, and even how to communicate among different generations! You'll discover powerful tips for making a great first impression, effective body language and the all-important follow-up.

The professionals you will meet in this book all want you to have quality tools and feel confident that you know how to make valuable connections. We have shared our best tips and provided proven guidelines that, when implemented, can turn you into a "networking ninja."

To get the most out of this book, we recommend that you read through it once, cover to cover. Then go back and follow the ideas that apply to you, in the chapters most relevant to your current situation. Every improvement you make in the way you network will make a difference in your business.

Becoming networking savvy can take some time. If you take action and apply the strategies, tips and tactics we share in these pages, you will reap many rewards. With our knowledge and your action, we are confident that, like our thousands of satisfied clients, you too will learn to *make your connections count.*

To you and your continued success!

The Co-Authors of *Make Your Connections Count*

First Impressions
You Can't Judge a Book by its Cover . . . or Can You?
By Mirella Zanatta

People often take things at face value. Within seconds of meeting you, they judge you based on your appearance and presence. Once you make these first impressions, they are nearly impossible to change. In *Blink: The Power of Thinking without Thinking* published by Little Brown and Company in 2005, Malcolm Gladwell concludes that, in this age of information overload, the experts often make better decisions with snap judgments than they do with volumes of analysis. Therefore, making a good first impression is important. I encourage you to take control of how people perceive you from those first moments of seeing you.

When we interact with each other, we constantly send and receive messages without speaking a word. Everything we do is a form of communication and everything we communicate leaves an impression. Eye contact, facial expressions, posture and gestures all contain subtle meanings.

There are three major reasons to be conscious of nonverbal behavior:

• Being aware of nonverbal behavior allows you to better receive messages.

• You will understand yourself better and become more conscious of signals that will reinforce—or negate—your message.

• Your communication experiences become clearer with improved interpretation and understanding.

Nonverbal communication is so significant that many psychiatrists, psychologists and researchers have devoted their entire lives to its study. Julius Fast popularized the lay term "body language" for nonverbal communication in 1970 with his book *Body Language,* most recently published by M. Evans and Company, Inc. in 2002 as a revised and updated edition.

The study of body movement, gestures and facial expressions is known as kinetics, while the study of pitch and tone of voice is known as paralanguage. These nonverbal signals are so powerful that a positive image can open doors and bring you respect, while a negative image causes people to doubt your ability. Unfortunately, countless people send negative or puzzling nonverbal signals without realizing it.

The good news is that much of our nonverbal communication is learned behavior, which means we can unlearn it and replace it with new behavior that serves us better. Unlocking the secret of exceptional conversation skills and first-rate people skills is a matter of strategy. Good communication skills can lay the foundation for success both personally and professionally, and can lead to a happy and rewarding life. Research has shown that the majority of our communication is nonverbal. Quite simply, it is not so much what you say—it is how you say it.

> *"By perseverance, study and eternal desire,*
> *any man can become great."*
> —George S. Patton, American officer, U.S. Army

Actions Speak Louder than Words

Use your entrance as an opportunity to create a great first impression. It is important to appear confident and approachable as you enter a room. An impeccable visual image sends a multitude of positive messages professionally, socially and personally. This attention to detail demonstrates that you have a command over the finer points of your life and that you will conduct business in the same manner.

Consistently demonstrate a powerful appearance whether you are in a business meeting, attending a black tie affair, exercising at the gym, grocery shopping or watching your child's soccer game. How many times have you left your house to run a quick errand hoping you would not run into anyone you know because you are not looking your best? You invariably end up seeing an acquaintance and then feel compelled to apologize for your appearance or you cower behind an aisle, hoping the person won't see you.

You represent your personal brand 24 hours a day. Take the extra five or ten minutes to make yourself presentable, and look forward to that unexpected encounter, impressing people with how you always look put-together.

The Eyes are the Windows of the Soul

Communication often begins with eye contact. It can signal interest and quickly convey a person's mood. Smiling, bright eyes indicate happiness or attraction. Cold, distant and hostile eyes suggest avoidance.

Eye contact can also be cultural. In North America, direct eye contact implies honesty and respect. In some cultures, people interpret it as disrespectful and challenging.

Looking down or away indicates you are not present or invested in the conversation. Someone may perceive you as a daydreamer, a shrinking violet or a wallflower. Instead, stand or sit up straight, taking up more space, and maintain eye contact to demonstrate a genuine interest. You will command more respect, establish a presence and make others feel more comfortable.

> *"There is no passion to be found playing small—in settling for a life that is less than the one you are capable of living."*
> —Nelson Mandela, anti-apartheid activist
> and former president of South Africa

A Picture Paints a Thousand Words

The human face is the most complex and highly developed of all species. It has the ability to express countless emotions such as happiness, sadness, anger, fear, surprise and disgust. These expressions are universal, making your behavior more predictable and understandable to others.

Your face—or as I like to call it the *canvas*—is the focal point of interest when you speak. You communicate with your colleagues more easily when you create a friendly atmosphere. Smiling is a powerful tool we often overlook. A smile can make you seem friendly and approachable. It is contagious. It will help put you and others at ease. Smile sincerely and try to be natural. People may perceive a forced smile as insincere.

Any part of your appearance that takes the attention away from your face serves as a distraction from what you say or do. Minimize your accessories in a business setting. Their size should be proportionate to your face and bone structure, and harmonious with your attire to create a polished look.

Yes, Mom Was Right

You may not want to hear this, but your mother was right: Good posture is important. Good posture not only makes you look taller and slimmer, it also has you appear more confident and credible. You communicate a wealth of information about yourself through your carriage. Congruence between your spoken word and your body language projects a powerful presence. This requires a clever balance of energy and experience. You do not want to appear over confident—or the opposite—too timid.

Body language is one of your most powerful tools. You do not have to go home and change your clothing to adjust your visual impact. The messages that your body language sends are subtle. For example, standing with your arms crossed over your chest implies being defensive or closed to the information you are receiving. Avoid placing your hands in your pockets. This can be distracting. Try to adopt a neutral position with your hands resting at your side. If you are seated at a table, place your hands, unclasped and visible on the table to evoke feelings of trust. You will appear approachable, open and relaxed, suggesting you are ready, aware of your environment, in control of your reactions and able to perform in the current circumstances.

Whether you are in a meeting with one person, delivering a presentation to a group or at a business networking function, you must always be sensitive to the messages you send. This knowledge will enable you to read your audience's responses and make any necessary adjustments.

Did He Just *Flip the Bird?*

We often express ourselves with gestures without being aware of them. We point and wave and often use our hands to animate our conversations. However, you may want to keep in mind that the meaning of certain gestures can be very different across cultures.

My background is Italian. In Italy, the *forefinger bite*—in which you place the knuckle of your bent forefinger between your teeth and symbolically bite it—means you are angry. My father was a man of few words, and the forefinger bite was just one of many messages he delivered without ever speaking a word. There was no need for a verbal translation.

Straight, sharp gestures, like pointing, can make you appear aggressive and intimidating. Smooth, curving gestures, like an open palm, make you appear more approachable, open, gentle and relaxed. Using your body language to project personal power increases your commanding presence, even when you are not dressed powerfully. Remember to be impeccably groomed and have well-manicured hands. Ladies, chipped nail polish can be a major distraction. It is better to wear no polish than to wear it chipped. As with jewelry and accessories, sometimes less is more.

Friends, Romans, Countrymen—Lend Me Your Ears

Listening is a terribly underestimated quality that requires your full concentration. Attentiveness and genuine interest are valuable qualities for successful interactions. It means not planning your response or daydreaming. Instead, be fully present in mind, body and thought. A totally engaged listener maintains eye contact, sometimes nods in agreement, and asks related questions.

Paraphrasing is a powerful tool. Essentially it is repetition—a recap of what you believe you heard in your own words. This allows the speaker to confirm your interpretation or further clarify his or her point. Observing the manner in which someone communicates will give you insight into how they best absorb information. Match and mirror your mannerisms and language style to the other person's mode and he or she is more likely to be receptive to your message. Good listeners have a knack for remembering names. Addressing someone by his or her name makes that person feel important and memorable. The best way to remember a name is to be genuinely interested in the person, listen closely while you are introduced and then reinforce the information by using the name in the conversation. Remembering names is an acquired skill. With practice it can be mastered.

> *"I like to listen. I have learned a great deal from listening carefully. Most people never listen."*
> —Ernest Hemingway, novelist

Would the Real *You* Please Stand Up?

Studies show that the majority of people in a business meeting experience anxiety. I suggest you be performance-driven, yet remain value-centered. Maintain integrity and honesty above all. A person of high ethics elevates standards by always doing the right thing, even when no one is looking. There is no room for two sets of behavior or manners, one for home and one while out in public. Think, act and look happy no matter what the environment. Be genuine or people will know you are faking it. Honor your commitment, tell the truth, respect others and always stand by your word. At the end of the day, you will be much happier for elevating your personal brand to such high standards. For more on being authentic, see *The Authentic Connection* by SherryLynn Wrenn and Sandra Fuentes on page 25.

I Am Delighted to Meet You

The handshake is the traditional way North Americans greet each other and we place much emphasis on it. Typically, it is the only point of physical contact we have with one another. We can tell a lot about a person by his or her handshake, therefore having a good one is important. Handshakes should be immediate and firm, yet not bone-crushing. Use web-to-web contact accompanied by good posture, direct eye contact and a sincere smile. We perceive the person who initiates the handshake as having more personal presence and confidence. In a business situation, it is proper to wait for the person of highest stature to initiate the handshake. Some cultures consider it improper for males and females to touch, replacing the handshake with a friendly nod.

Close, but No Cigar

To get people to listen when you speak, scrutinize your tone, pitch, volume, inflection and rate. Are people ignoring you or asking you to repeat yourself? This may be a telltale sign you are speaking too softly, mumbling or speaking too quickly. Loud speakers may attract attention; however they probably receive that attention for being obnoxious and overbearing.

Practice speaking clearly both in tone and in volume. Make a point to enunciate your words. Take your time speaking, as it will make you appear more thoughtful. It can help to videotape yourself to determine your strengths and weaknesses. This can be a valuable exercise, especially if you have no idea how you come across to others.

Break a Leg

Creating your personal brand is largely determined by how you behave in public. Networking events can be uncomfortable or intimidating. Do not despair. Engaging in enjoyable conversations with strangers does not have to be a daunting task. Keep in mind others may be experiencing the same butterflies you are.

Try to arrive early or at the beginning of an event. It is much easier to navigate the room with fewer people present. Odds are some people may be still waiting for their friends to arrive, and they are also looking for someone to talk to. To strike up conversation, smile, then make eye contact and introduce yourself. You may tell them what brought you to the event, or ask them how they know the host. Choose positive topics such as movies, shows, plays, documentaries, recent news, travel or their interests. Even the weather can be a great icebreaker.

To appear more cosmopolitan and well informed, do a little research before you head out. This can be as simple as a few clicks—the Internet brings the world to us through videos, blogs, podcasts and educational sites. Be courteous to everyone, saying please and thank you. Listen attentively, smile and show an authentic interest.

To meet as many people as possible at networking events, limit each conversation to five to ten minutes. Politely disengage by telling them how much you enjoyed meeting them, exchange business cards if you want additional contact and then move on and repeat the process. See *How to Attract More Clients Through Effective Networking* by PJ Van Hulle on page 133 for more on this subject.

Bite Your Tongue

Avoid filler words such as *uh, um, like, you know.* Also avoid buzz words, slang or jargon. Steer clear of discussions about money, such as how much something cost or how much money you make. Do not gossip, boast, swear, name drop, criticize, complain, condescend, give unsolicited advice or say anything controversial. Politics and religion have the potential to get emotional—steer clear of those topics. Refrain from asking questions like, "What do you do? Where are you from? Where did you go to school?" Avoid personal comments about age or marital status. These are superficial questions used to identify status and may also pose legal implications in a business setting. Such topics may come up in longer conversations. However, they are not good starting points.

Take Your Foot Out of Your Mouth

Sometimes we become angry, stressed, overwhelmed or anxious. These emotions can compromise even our best intentions. When these circumstances present themselves—and they will—remember to breathe. Inhale slowly through your nose and exhale through your mouth. Try to regain your equilibrium. Choose your words carefully so you can deal with the situation in a positive way.

In a heated discussion, stick to the facts and do not make personal remarks or judgments. If someone is upset, respond calmly with, "I'm sorry you feel that way." This validates their right to their feelings, yet does not necessarily mean you agree with them. Believe in the law of attraction—train your mind to think about what you want to see happen as opposed to what you do not want. Stress happens when you pay attention to the wrong things. Visualize the outcome that you want and make it a habit to expect things to run smoothly. You will begin to feel more confident and get better results because people will respond differently to you.

Flexibility is an important weapon in your arsenal. People respond differently to the same words. Adapt your approach depending on your audience. The secret is to observe the way they speak to you. It is usually the way they like to be spoken to.

What Do You Want Your Image to Say?

How do you want people to see you? Poised, charming, charismatic, capable, successful, confident and respected are all powerful and attractive qualities within your reach. With a decisive mind-set, candid self-awareness and clear objectives combined with a positive, professional image, you can have a distinct competitive advantage. By mastering the necessary skills of image management, verbal communication and body language, you will find it easy to create a great first impression every time. Are you prepared to do the work? The choice is yours!

MIRELLA ZANATTA
First Impressions Image Consulting

Inspiring you to achieve greatness

(519) 473-2396
mz@firstimpressionsimageconsulting.com
www.firstimpressionsimageconsulting.com

In her early 30s Mirella Zanatta was living her dream. Married to her high school sweetheart, she had two beautiful children and a career she loved. In the blink of an eye her life changed forever after her car collided with a truck. Her husband was killed, she sustained physical and emotional injuries, and was left to pick up the pieces and move forward into a future she had not chosen. Physically unable to resume her teaching career, she stayed home to raise her children, embarking on a long personal journey to achieve spiritual consciousness, which she found to be essential to her personal happiness.

Once her children were grown, Mirella searched for what was next. She realized that being an image consultant combined her teaching and counseling skills with her flair for fashion and the innate sense of style she inherited from her mother, a fashion stylist and master tailor.

Mirella's background in retail fashion, education and counseling, along with her communication and public speaking skills, make her a sought after image professional. A graduate of the International Image Institute, she is an active member of the Association of Image Consultants International (AICI) and serves on the board of the AICI Canada Chapter.

Professional Presence and Visual Impact

Look and Feel Your Best to Make Great Connections

By Lori Barber

You have the potential to network or connect with people socially or professionally whenever you are in public. Your public perception is your introduction to the world and conveys information about you—from your skills, talents and education level to your capacity for organization, creativity or leadership.

You have a very small window in which to make the best impression on meaningful connections. Your appearance is a powerful tool that immediately speaks volumes about you—a picture is worth a thousand words. You have five to ten minutes to make an impression, stand out, differentiate yourself, convey your message and be your best. A powerful and professional image and consistent, positive body language are essential for making a good impression.

Think of your image as a beautiful frame around a piece of artwork. The artwork represents you, your experiences, your current position and your skills. It symbolizes the time and effort you have made to research the client's needs, study the corporation or prepare for a presentation. The frame showcases the art and readies it for public display. The frame represents your visual appearance, body language and behavior. It must send an authentic message that enhances the meaning of the artwork.

In a networking scenario, you can control three things:

- **What people hear:** your words, your tone of voice

- **What people perceive:** your authenticity, grace, etiquette and integrity

- **What people see:** your appearance—your attire, body language and overall presence

These tell your story as a person. They need to match the message you are sending. You will differentiate yourself and give yourself an edge in the workplace if you validate yourself through your image and visual impact.

> *"A strong, positive self-image is the best possible preparation for success in life."*
> —Dr. Joyce Brothers, American psychologist
> and television personality

Top Three Reasons to Focus on Professional Image when Networking

Reinforce your message. Communication goes beyond words. It includes your tone of voice, body language, behavior and visual appearance. Does your image communicate "sloppy, boring and outdated," or "polished, creative and current?"

The secret to making connections is communicating effectively. Your image speaks volumes about who you are and who you want to be. Imagine the CEO of a quirky, creative and cutting-edge company speaking to his new sales force in a stuffy, boring suit. This conflicts with his desired message of current and cool—his audience may tune out and not listen to his presentation.

Increase confidence. Networking can be challenging. Being confident in front of hiring managers, new clients or an audience is difficult enough without worrying about your attire. Confidence is a belief in oneself and one's abilities. It is a crucial factor in achieving your personal and professional goals. Knowing who you are and representing yourself authentically increases self-confidence and self-esteem.

> *"Giving people self-confidence is by far the most important thing that I can do. Because then they will act."*
> —Jack Welch, American chemical engineer,
> businessman and author

Differentiate yourself. In the *Harvard Business Review Blog* article "Do You Pass the Leadership Test?," published August 3, 2010, William C. Taylor, co-founder of *Fast Company* magazine, wrote "It's not good enough to be 'pretty good' at everything today. You have to be the most of something: the most elegant, the most colorful, the most responsive, the most focused." This helps you stand out from the crowd. For more on this subject, see *Use Speaking to Build a Thriving Network* by Caterina Rando on page 209.

Pay attention to how you put yourself together. As highlighted in the July 2010 Forbes.com article, "What Not to Wear to Work," Carol Hymowitz writes, ". . . in a world where jobs are few and far between, never has office attire been as important as it is now." Dress for success every day regardless of your agenda—you never know when the perfect opportunity will arise to advance your career.

Five Tips to Increase Success with Appearance and Dress

By upgrading your level of professional presence and image, you gain credibility and showcase your competence in the workplace.

Update. One top item that can rob credibility is an outdated suit or outfit. I worked with a client who wanted to increase sales and gain new clients for his business. He wore ten-year-old suits. He dressed for who he was ten years ago—not who he is today or who he wants to become. His confidence—and client base—soared when we put him in a new suit, modern dress shirt and tie. When your image says contemporary and modern, not dated and old-fashioned, people are drawn to your message and your company.

Fit. People commonly wear clothing either too big or too small. Either of these actually makes you appear heavier than you are. Excellent clothing fit is a sign of elegance and helps you appear slimmer and taller. Imagine a CFO interviewing for a financial position that requires attention to detail and organizational skills in order to impart a level of trust with clients. If that CFO arrives wearing an ill-fitting suit and a disheveled look, the hiring manager may assume he or she is not detailed and organized enough to handle the job.

Quality. I gave a presentation to some executives in job transition. After the presentation, a gentleman approached me and asked what I thought of his image. He was pursuing a career in the private equity business, looking for major funding from banks and corporations. I noticed his frayed belt and scuffed shoes. This gave the impression he did not know how to manage money or invest in his most important asset—himself. You are your most important asset. I encourage you to invest in the highest quality business clothing you can afford.

Color. Color can make a powerful statement and you can use color to your advantage. Colors like navy blue and charcoal grey convey authority or power. You can showcase your creativity by using touches of orange or purple. Color affects us physically, mentally and emotionally. It can convey sincerity, friendliness, trustworthiness and positive energy. To be more approachable at work, avoid all black and add more color to your wardrobe. To stand out and be remembered at a crowded networking event or during a presentation, wear bold and bright colors near your face.

Details. If you feel frumpy or boring, or if you are not getting noticed at events, wear classy accessories to add personality, interest and excitement to your business wardrobe. A woman can add a beautiful necklace and earring set to pick up the colors in her silk blouse—a man can add a luxurious leather belt, shoes and briefcase to show the world he cares about his image. Pay attention to your hair, hands and teeth. Carry an engraved business card holder, fine pen or soft leather money clip.

> *"It's the little details that are vital.*
> *Little things make big things happen."*
> —John Wooden, American basketball player and coach

Five Tips to Increase Success with Body Language and Behavior

In the book *Everyone Communicates, Few Connect,* published by Thomas Nelson in 2010, leadership expert John C. Maxwell writes, "More than ninety percent of the impression we often convey has nothing to do with what we actually say."

Our intellect and our words are important, yet our body language, tone of voice and appearance speak volumes. If I tell you that I am pleased to meet you, yet I do not make eye contact and I am focused on something else, my body language directly conflicts with what I am saying. You are more likely to believe my body language than my words. Follow these tips to make a great first impression.

Smile. When you enter a room, give a presentation or meet new people, smile. I smile when I give presentations and I always have the whole room smiling back at me. This reinforces my message: I am happy to be here, and I am friendly and approachable. Project positive energy and "good vibrations."

Eye contact. When I coach people for interviews, I suggest they maintain eye contact for ten seconds longer than is comfortable. I also make eye contact during presentations to connect with my audience and show them I am present and engaged. When you make eye contact with people, you make personal connections that contribute to your overall networking goals.

Integrity. Recently, I have been hearing many stories about lack of integrity in the workplace. Have you heard a tasteless joke at work and felt uncomfortable? Has someone promised you something that you counted on and then never came through? Has someone unfairly blamed you for something? These are examples of a lack of integrity.

Do not burn bridges in business. Adhere to your moral principles. Deal with people fairly. Accept responsibility for your mistakes.

Listen. I have been practicing the art of authentic listening with my kids. In my busy life, I have the tendency to continue with my projects while my kids are trying to tell me something that is important to them. I remind myself to stop what I am doing, look them in the eyes and try to really understand what they are saying to me. This is authentic listening. You can also use this in business. Whether you are on the phone or meeting in person, stop what you are doing, focus on the person's voice or eyes and really listen and understand what he or she says. This will make you feel more connected in all of your relationships.

Etiquette. As Peggy and Peter Post wrote in their book, *The Etiquette Advantage in Business,* 2nd Edition, published in 2005 by William Morrow, as the "workplace becomes increasingly more competitive, knowing how to behave can make the difference between getting ahead and getting left behind." This is a good reminder of what our parents taught us: Say please and thank you, mind your manners, do not talk behind someone's back and do not underestimate the power of a handwritten thank you note.

"Etiquette is a code of behavior based on honesty,
respect and consideration."
—www.emilypost.com

Three Networking Scenarios and What to Wear for Each

It is important to understand levels of business dress and how to be appropriate for different events and experiences. Follow these guidelines to ensure that your image matches your event.

Professional. This includes interviews, formal presentation or public speaking, as well as important client and manager meetings. Think "subtle, simple and polished." Most interviews and high-level client meetings call for formal business dress. This is a great time to showcase your professionalism. In a creative industry, you may have more leeway in your dress. However, always remember to keep business first. For second interviews, or if you are clearly instructed to wear business casual attire, see the Business Casual section below.

Men: A great-fitting business suit is the foundation of a man's wardrobe. Invest in a classic, two-button jacket suit in a Super 100 wool or high-quality wool blend in navy or charcoal. I like a subtle pinstripe or plaid. I advise my clients to avoid the harsh look of black.

To stay up-to-date, it may be time to invest in a new suit if your suit is five years old or older. Modernize your button-down collar shirt to an elegant, wide-spread or point-collar, fine cotton herringbone shirt. Look for white, light blue or a subtle pattern. Combine your new suit and shirt with a bold or bright tie to complement them.

Finish off the elegant look with leather wing tips or lace-up shoes with a matching belt, quality leather briefcase and a beautiful watch.

Women: A pantsuit, skirted suit or sheath dress with a jacket is a classic look for any corporate occasion. Skirts should hit at or just below the knee. Always wear a jacket to gain credibility and respect. In addition to classic navy, grey and black, try burgundy, dark green or chocolate brown.

Do not be afraid to use a colorful silk blouse, a chic necklace or an elegant leather tote to look pretty and professional. Avoid clutter by bringing a purse or briefcase—not both. Wear pantyhose with a closed-toe, modern, two-inch leather pump for a formal interview.

Business casual. This is for a job search networking meeting, trade association meeting, business travel, conference or seminar. The key to keeping business casual attire from being "business catastrophe attire" is to think business first and casual second. This level of dress gives you a great opportunity to stand out from the underdressed crowd by looking professional, appropriate and approachable.

Men: A suit without a tie is appropriate here. This is your chance to bypass the rumpled khakis in favor of a mid- to lightweight wool slack in black, grey, navy, tan, khaki or olive. Pair it with a silk/wool blend sport coat in tweed, windowpane, herringbone or houndstooth. Airport travel, business conferences and luncheon meetings are great places to make connections, and business casual attire is the perfect choice for these occasions. Do not waste the opportunity by showing up in your weekend casual clothes.

Women: Add separates to your wardrobe for the perfect business casual look. Look for pencil and a-line skirts, classic trousers, sheath and shirt dresses, collared blouses, cardigans and casual jackets with fun details and color. I teach my clients about wardrobe capsules to save them time and money in their closets. Follow these four, easy tips to make dressing and shopping a breeze.

- **Pick your colors.** Pick two neutrals and one accent color, such as navy blue, cream and plum.

- **Choose your fabrics.** For a business wardrobe, stick with natural, dressier fabrics, such as gabardine or worsted wool, tweed, silk, rayon or cotton.

- **Pick a style.** For a put-together look, stick with one or two styles— the best style for business is classic trend or classic elegant.

- **Choose accessories.** Here's the fun part—find scarves, shoes, belts, jewelry and leather handbags in coordinating colors!

Social. This includes after-hours networking, semi-formal events, dinner parties or luncheon meetings. In social situations, you can relax the business dress and add fun and trendy colors, accessories or styles. However, always keep it appropriate—you just may run into that important contact!

Men: A black suit in the evening is always a big yes! Depending on the event, you can vary your business day look by trying a silk polo shirt under a suit, or a white dress shirt, red cashmere sweater vest and black sport coat with grey wool trousers. Dark jeans and an elegant sport coat with leather slip-on shoes always look great at those more casual social events.

Women: Shed the business classic pieces and add details like sequins, sparkly jewelry, silk wraps or strappy shoes to look more festive. Remember to avoid cleavage and short skirts in a business social setting.

Get Ready to Make That Great First Impression

Do you walk in a room with your head held high, a smile on your face and in a fantastic outfit? Are you dressed for your dream job, or dressed for the job you had ten years ago? When you network to progress your career and to make connections for success, frame yourself in a positive way to reinforce the message you want to send.

After reading these tips and guidelines, create a professional image that will contribute to your success. Invest in a new suit or classic business wardrobe pieces. An image consultant can help you understand your colors, style and the best silhouette for your body type. Assess the clothes that you have in your wardrobe and update those that need it.

Understand your professional image. Invest in yourself to increase your confidence, reinforce your message and differentiate yourself in the marketplace.

LORI BARBER
Elements Image Consulting

(404) 310-3700
lori@elementsimage.com
www.elementsimage.com

Lori Barber, president of Elements Image Consulting, provides clients with elements of style, confidence and success to enrich their daily lives and align their public image with their personal and professional goals. She offers personalized professional presence and image management consultations and is a successful presenter and coach in corporate workshops, seminars and style boot camps.

Lori is certified with the internationally-renowned London Image Institute® in professional development, personal branding and image management—including color, style, wardrobe analysis, body language and communication skills. She is a member of the Association of Image Consultants International and serves on the board of the Atlanta Chapter of AICI.

Before starting her business, Lori had more than a decade of experience working in Fortune 100 companies, including Westinghouse Electric Corporation, Eaton Corporation and UUNET/MCI Worldcom Company. Her positions included national accounts manager, regional marketing manager and channel account executive. Lori excelled in sales, marketing, training and partner relationships. With her extensive corporate background, and training in image, professional presence and personal branding, Lori is uniquely positioned to help you take your image to the next level and meet your personal and professional goals.

The Authentic Connection
By SherryLynn Wrenn and Sandra Fuentes

Sometimes we walk through life doing other people's bidding. We take what others say as right or good for us and make that our life's plan. We do not define what success means to *us*. This comes from not being confident in ourselves and in what we have chosen to do. When we doubt who we are and continue on paths that are not our own, we get results that mean something to other people and not to ourselves. In addition, we may never be content with our achievements.

How do you get to your own destination? The answer is simple: You create your own path. Then you will not only get to where you truly want to be in life, you will also be happier in your choices.

As you read this chapter, I recommend that you make lists and put your ideas in writing. This will help you see, read and analyze your thoughts more effectively. It will give you something concrete with which to move forward.

> *"We need to find the courage to say no to the things and people that are not serving us if we want to rediscover ourselves and live our lives with authenticity."*
> —Barbara De Angelis, PhD, American author
> and motivational speaker

Create Your Own Path

What makes your business a reflection of you? No matter what business you are in, you must make it unique to you and a reflection of your goals. Of course you can use methods of success from those you admire. However, the challenge is for you to create your own niche.

Let's say you attended a training seminar where the speaker was wildly energizing and shared fantastic ideas. You promised yourself to be more like her in order to achieve the same success she has. Something happens—you feel uncomfortable and cannot generate the enthusiasm she demonstrated. Her personality is not what you need to model—it is her *ideas*. Take her ideas and mold them to fit your personality.

Instead of focusing on how that dynamic speaker is not like you, listen to the fabulous ideas she had. Think about what you want from your business and consider your personal needs and desires—not those of others. What are ten things that you want from your business?

How to Discover Your Authentic Self

> *"Never mind searching for who you are.*
> *Search for the person you aspire to be."*
> —Robert Brault, American writer

The greatest gift you can give to yourself is to be truly authentic. This is also the single most valuable resource you can share with others. Authenticity within yourself is a work in progress most of the time and you can define it. Discovering our authenticity requires us to address the following three questions. We have also included some possible answers to get you started.

1. What traits do successful people possess?

- Self-motivation

- Positive attitude

- Financial stability

- Commitment

- Happiness

2. What do you need in your life to be successful?

- Love

- Peace

- Abundance

3. What do you need from others to be successful?

- Dedication

- Support

- Their time

Part of finding your authenticity is building an awareness of the traits successful people possess, and those that have meaning for you. Answer the first question above by writing down ten traits you believe are important for a successful individual to possess.

Recognizing what you want from your life is an important aspect of finding your authentic self.

In your search for authenticity, you may overlook what you expect from others. If you expect others to complete important tasks for you, you are not being authentic in your expectations because you cannot control what others do or think—only how you react to them. Often, what you expect from others reflects what you need to give to others. If you expect it, why would others not expect the same things from you? Now answer the second and third questions from page 26 and write down ten things you feel you need from others to be successful.

Combine your list of ten traits with your list of ten things you believe you need in your life to be successful, and you will have a clear map of who you want to be. This is your path to authenticity.

Once you visualize a picture of your authentic self, you can create that person. This can be an exciting and empowering process, as you give yourself the freedom to live your life from a genuine place. This, in turn, gives you confidence and adds value to the relationships you have with others.

The most important thing to remember when you are becoming your authentic self is honesty. You need to be honest with yourself in what you expect from yourself, your life and others. We suggested that you make a list of the traits that are important to you and examine them. Do you have these traits? If not, you have some things to work on. Make an investment in yourself and take time to be sure you are doing what you think is most valuable. If your list validates that you are already living your life with these traits, you are well on your way to developing your authentic connections.

Attaining Success through Authentic Connections

> *"The way we communicate with others and with ourselves
> ultimately determines the quality of our lives."*
> –Tony Robbins, American entrepreneur, speaker and author

Now it is time to concentrate on success. A part of being honest with yourself is being clear about what you want from your business. The word success comes from a Latin word meaning "an outcome." That is broad, isn't it? You have a whole world open to you to define what success means to you, and you are its creator in your life. Being clear is critical to achieving it.

Sit in a quiet area and think of all your dreams and goals in life. Write down your perfect vision of your success. What you see on that piece of paper is what you are trying to achieve. You can have it if you do business from a place of authenticity.

> *"Always be a first-rate version of yourself,*
> *instead of a second-rate version of somebody else."*
> —Judy Garland, American actor and entertainer

Developing Relationships of Choice

Once you have discovered what you want from yourself, from others and within your business, you can then develop dependable and pure relationships with people you choose to have in your life.

You do not have to develop a deep and personal relationship with every person who enters your life. Let's use the image of a ladder to portray those in your life. On this ladder to a successful business, you meet others. How you relate to them and do business with them determines how far this ladder can reach.

People do business with people they like and trust. If you are not true to yourself, it is difficult to garner support. Without a vision on which to focus, the other people in your life don't have an easy way to support you.

Look at the ladder as a stepping-stone to the relationships you forge with others. Each time someone achieves one of the rungs on the ladder—supporters, networkers and partners—they move up to the next level of relationship with you. That is your ultimate goal when building connections—to climb the ladder side by side. Alone is just that—alone. For more on developing relationships, see *Set Yourself Apart by Doing the Little Things* by Jenny Bywater on page 99.

> *"The ladder of success is best climbed by stepping on the rungs of opportunity."*
> —Ayn Rand, Russian-American novelist, philosopher, playwright and screenwriter

Supporters. You start out with supporters. They are the people on whom you initially rely to get your business off the ground—family, friends and your initial clients. They are an important part of this ladder, holding it firmly to the ground and making sure it does not fall.

You cultivate relationships with supporters by being honest with them. You tell them what you plan to do, and you do it. You give them what you have promised and follow up with them. These people will trust you to lead the way. You are the expert and the one making the promises. To solidify that bond, you must deliver.

Many people make the mistake of expecting more from their supporters. Remember, it is your job to create trust. It is your responsibility to show them that doing business with you has value. You expect nothing more from them than allowing you that opportunity.

When you show your supporters they can depend on you, they may move up to the next rung on your ladder. To keep the foundation of your ladder strong, continue to bring new supporters in and nourish the supporters you have.

Networkers. Some of your supporters will move up your ladder to be networkers. These people know they can rely on you for the services you provide. They know you will give them your time and are focused on their best interests. They will pay this forward by sharing you with others. You can invite people onto the networkers rung without previous business interaction with them. However, they will be much more consistent and passionate about what you have to offer if you have already built a relationship with them.

Your networkers are people you can actively seek out. Other business owners are ideal as they have an abundant list of contacts they can share with you. Cross-promotion with these connections is a valuable way to grow your business. When you have developed trust, they will send their clientele to you knowing you will treat them with the same professional kindness.

Always allow your networkers to refer you to others and give them the ability to do so. Offer them incentives for their clients and fulfill those promotions efficiently. Provide them with business cards, promotional material and their own referral bonus. This will ensure they remember you when someone they know needs your service.

There is power in numbers. Having the illusion you can do it all on your own is just that—an illusion.

"Achievement is not the most important thing—authenticity is."
—Author Unknown

Partners. Sometimes, an amazing thing occurs with your supporters and networkers. They want to become a part of your business. Once you have established and recognized your supporters and networkers, you will find that business partners start appearing. The next rung on your ladder represents your partners.

Your partners are people with whom you have created a bona fide business relationship—those with whom you have formed the closest connections. You have proven your authenticity to them time after time, and they are there for you. This does not always mean they work for you or within your business. It means they work with you. When they join you in this partnership, magic happens.

Your business partners will include your employees, coworkers and mentors. Remember, viewing them as partners gives you an advantage.

Human nature dictates that conflicts will arise. This is especially true when it comes to those with whom you work closely—your business partners. Recovering from conflicts with partners can be difficult if you have not established solutions before the fallout. Plan your response ahead of time.

Conducting business without looking at some of the things that can go wrong is a critical error. There will be bumps in the road—knowing how you will counter them will save you time, emotion and energy. This also shows your business partners your limits. When they are aware of how you plan to deal with a given situation, you can often avoid the problem altogether.

When you have built that authentic relationship, others are aware of how you do business and respond to conflict. They respect your views and your methods. For example, let's say your partner feels as if you have not shown enough appreciation for what he or she has done for you. Are you prepared to take this on authentically or will you avoid it at all costs? How you perceive something may not be someone else's perception. You need to do your best to make sure your perceptions match as closely as possible. You may feel you have given your partner enough recognition for his or her contribution. Ask yourself if this is your definition of recognition or your partner's. Comparing the two may give you a clearer vision of how to respond.

Let your partners know they can share their concerns with you. This is important in developing your relationships. Your ability to take care of those concerns from a professional and authentic place will ensure continued support from your partners.

All Work and No Play

"Play has been man's most useful preoccupation."
—Frank Caplan, American toy creator, author and educator

Take time to do the things you love. Your business is a huge part of your life. However, it does not identify who you are as a person. You need to have time to nurture your authenticity. Otherwise, you will not effectively relate to others.

Periodically take the time to remind yourself of why you started this whole venture in the first place. This will help you stay focused and stay on the path of success.

Make time for you, your family and your friends away from your business. This is crucial in finding balance. When you are clear on who you are in everyday life, you will be much more equipped to maintain that balance.

Now is your time! You have all the answers. This chapter did not give them to you–you have found them yourself.

Use the questions in this chapter to help discover your authentic self. Make your connections count by creating your own path and developing the relationships you choose. We believe that when you take time to be honest with yourself and discover that you need to be in charge of your own destiny, you will find the authentic success that is the core of your authentic self. Why would you choose anything less?

SANDRA FUENTES
Passion Parties®
(403)331-3662
idohair@telus.net
www.sandraspassion.com

SHERRYLYNN WRENN
Passion Parties®
(780) 446-8118
shers_passion@shaw.ca
www.sherspassion.com

Sandra and SherryLynn are Passion Parties® business partners in Alberta, Canada. Sandra is a wife, mother of three children and a breast cancer survivor. She is known for her tireless efforts in the fight against the disease. SherryLynn is a wife and the mother of two sons and spent many years as a stay-at-home mom. She "developed an attitude problem" about going back to work and decided to become her own boss.

Sandra and SherryLynn were friends first and then business partners who grew a close connection through their journey together. They learned if they wanted to be successful together, they had to be honest with and supportive of each other—no matter what. They balance friendship and business with ease by being their authentic selves. If one has a bad day, the other steps up to lead.

Sandra enjoys many crafts, such as card-making and scrapbooking. SherryLynn prefers movies and spending time with her boys. They are committed to working together to make their businesses thrive and grow while keeping one another grounded and authentic.

Make Your Connections Count Across Generations

By Bruce Bright, LtCol USMC (Ret), CCIM, CPC

*D*o you want to increase your bottom line? By implementing a few simple steps to create more effective communications and better connections among generations in the workplace, you can start seeing results today!

Most organizations have peak performers at every level. You may have these superstars working throughout your organization. However, they may not communicate well with each other. This can affect relationships, teamwork and the bottom line.

Imagine an organization in which peak performers have daily targets they consistently hit. For each of them, that looks like Diagram 1. The CEO of this organization has five divisions, all with team members hitting individual targets. However, his Organizational Target looks like Diagram 2. The key to getting the organization to be on target is to connect all of the employees through effective communications as in Diagram 3.

Employee View   Employer View   After Training

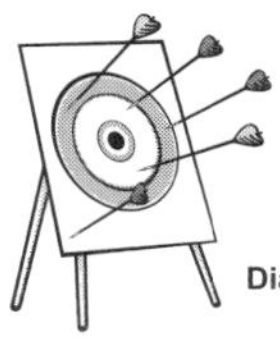

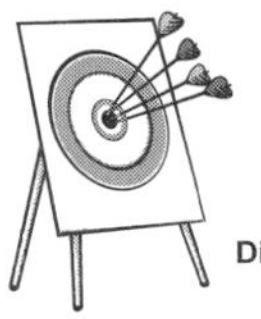

Diagram 1   Diagram 2   Diagram 3

Have you encountered a situation in which a better method of communication could have helped you avoid a confrontation, saving you time, a relationship or money? Worse than poor communication is no communication or no communication method.

According to a 2009-2010 multi-regional study report conducted by Towers Watson®, a leading global professional services company, "Effective employee communication is a leading indicator of financial performance and a driver of employee engagement. Companies that are highly effective communicators had 47 percent higher total returns to shareholders over the last five years compared with firms that are the least effective communicators."

Understanding how people from different generations think allows for better communication. When everyone understands each other, you can get the whole organization on target and help increase your bottom line.

> *"To effectively communicate, we must realize that we are all different in the way we perceive the world and use this understanding as a guide to our communication with others."*
> —Tony Robbins, American entrepreneur, speaker and author

Consider this scenario: A baby boomer CEO gives a Generation Y employee a handwritten note with instructions to handle a task. The employee sees this as an ancient a way to communicate. When she completes the assignment, she instant messages (IMs) her boss she is finished. The CEO does not IM and, therefore, is unaware the employee has completed the job. The employee would like recognition on a job well done and probably will not receive it in a timely fashion, if at all. The CEO would give recognition if he only knew that the task was complete. However, neither will get what they want or need in this situation.

Both the CEO and the employee are frustrated due to lack of communication. The time, effort and wasted energy necessary to correct the issue will affect the company's bottom line—especially if this scenario replays itself across the entire organization.

Most generations want to communicate better. With a little education, they can help each other get on target. We currently have four generations in the workplace. Let's take a look at each generation, what influenced their lives and their values, what they like and dislike and how best to communicate with them.

The Greatest Generation

> *"Use it up, wear it out, make it do, or do without."*
> —World War II poster and motto of the Greatest Generation

The Greatest Generation (GGs) was born between 1901 and 1925 and still influences America. Tom Brokaw coined the term in his book, *The Greatest Generation,* published by Random House in 1998. Their parents' values date back to experiences in the 1800s. The GGs lived through the Great Depression and World War II, both of which made them tough and resourceful. They grew up with little resources and had no phone service, Internet or television in their formative years. Automobiles were scarce and the road system was lacking. They sacrificed time with their families to fight in World War II during their young adult lives.

Now in their 80s and 90s, the GGs bring many assets to their relationships. They have proven experience and knowledge, are loyal, consistent and fair, and have stable lives. They respect authority and prefer direct leaders and logical approaches to opportunities. They have no problem working for someone younger, yet they do expect leaders who are respectful. You can motivate GGs by recognizing their experience and their perseverance over so many years. They like tangible symbols of loyalty, commitment and service, including plaques and certificates.

GGs like leaders who use a personal touch to communicate—memos, handwritten letters and personal notes—and prefer not to connect via computer. They want younger people to be mindful of their age and experience and want to become a mentor to them.

GGs do *not* appreciate:

• "Touchy-feely" or indecisive leaders

• Disorganized leaders

• Profanity or slang

Lastly, GGs tend to be outspoken and honest and do not try to impress people. They have "been there and done that"—and did it well!

Action Steps for More Effective Communication with the Greatest Generation:

• Be respectful of their age and experience.

• Use handwritten notes, memos and letters, and communicate face to face.

• Do not use slang or profanity.

• Be direct, yet fair and consistent.

• Use them as mentors.

The Silent Generation

"Now in our 60s and 70s, we've finally reached the teenage rebellion stage!"
—Frank Kaiser, American columnist

The label "Silent Generation" was first coined in the November 5, 1951 cover story of *Time* magazine in which reporters stated, "Youth today is waiting for the hand of fate to fall on its shoulders, meanwhile working fairly hard and saying almost nothing. The most startling fact about the younger generation is its silence. With some rare exceptions, youth is nowhere near the rostrum. By comparison with the flaming youth of their fathers and mothers, today's younger generation is a still, small flame. It does not issue manifestos, make speeches or carry posters. It has been called the 'Silent Generation.'"

The Silent Generation (SGs) was born between 1926 and 1944. Many of the younger members are still in the workforce and the older ones still influence the workforce. They lived in the shadow of their hero parents. The SGs served in the Korean War and Vietnam.

Older SGs tend to follow the Greatest Generation stereotypes, and younger SGs tend to fit in with Baby Boomers. To more effectively communicate with older members of the Silent Generation, follow the action steps for the Greatest Generation—when communicating with the youngest SGs, follow the action steps for the Baby Boomers listed below.

Baby Boomers

"The message may not move me, or mean a great deal to me, but hey, it feels so groovy to say ... I dig rock 'n' roll music ... "
—Peter, Paul & Mary, American folk singers

Baby Boomers (BBs) are generally considered to be born between 1945 and 1962. When births increased in post war America, columnist Sylvia Porter used the term "boom" in the *New York Post* in reference to this occurrence.

They are today's American leaders. They are the children of the rough-and-tough Greatest Generation, and most grew up in a two-parent home. GGs wanted their children to have better lives, and the abundant treatment from their parents resulted in the beginning of what has been called the "Me" generation.

BBs grew up knowing what their parents had endured, and they value climbing the ladder of success. Many like being part of large organizations and are responsible for the term "workaholic." BBs prefer unlimited possibilities and constant change. They do not like rules and regulations and they challenge authority. BBs like to work in groups if others perform at their level, and much prefer a democratic approach to problems. They tend to avoid the command and control style of leadership their parents used.

BBs like to work for consensual leaders who are willing to hear and agree with their ideas. The members of this group listen to others, yet challenge ideas and ask for details.

Speak to BBs openly and directly, without trying to control them. They want you to like their ideas and are not good with bureaucratic or harsh direction. Give them options that show your flexibility and be willing to give them input. To motivate BBs, get them involved and let them know you need them.

BBs can use most forms of communication. However, many are more likely to prefer personal interaction. They are comfortable with technology, like flexible working arrangements, company-provided health and wellness programs and personal time.

Action Steps for More Effective Communication with the Baby Boomer Generation:

• Be open to their ideas and show interest in them.

• Use personal interaction.

• Get them involved at all levels of the plan.

• Use a democratic approach to solving problems.

Generation X

> *"When someone tells you they've just bought a house, they might as well tell you they no longer have a personality. You can immediately assume so many things: that they're locked into jobs they hate; that they're broke; that they spend every night watching videos; that they're fifteen pounds overweight; that they no longer listen to new ideas. It's profoundly depressing."*
> —Douglas Coupland, Canadian fiction writer
> and cultural commentator

Generation Xers (GenXers) are generally considered to be born between 1963 and 1980. They are also called the "Baby Busters" because of the declining birth rate compared to BBs. They have the "X" designation because they do not feel like they fit in anywhere. They live in the shadow of the Baby Boomers. This generation saw their parents struggle with being laid off from work, the rise of feminism and skyrocketing divorce rates.

Many GenXers grew up in single-parent homes or with working mothers in two-parent homes, causing them to become independent, self-reliant and resourceful. Now in their thirties and forties, they want independence in the workplace. GenXers will send out resumes and take the next best job offer when things are not going well or their way. Company loyalty is not something they value.

They are more loyal to themselves, their projects and their partners on the project than to the organization. GenXers are not interested in climbing the corporate ladder. Instead, they have their own networks where they can climb up, over, down or diagonally. This generation grew up while technology was changing at a previously unmatched rate. They require the latest technology at work and prefer to complete assignments in their own way and on their own schedule. If they are micro-managed, they will just move on to another opportunity.

GenXers are extremely flexible. They work to live, as opposed to the BBs style of living to work. GenXers value free time, demand that employers allow fun at work and believe work should not get in the way of fun—both can happen successfully. They complete their work above expectations to leave plenty of time for fun with their friends. Employers who understand this can command the best of GenXers, while organizations that refuse to accommodate fun at work will lose wonderful talent to the competition.

They like straightforward leaders who are genuine, flexible, informal and results-oriented. They want training and growth opportunities to prepare for that next position. GenXers take any assignment and run with it, needing little supervision, and their results are impressive.

GenXers are *not* happy with:

• Micro-managing leaders

• Leaders who do not walk their talk

• Bureaucrats who place more importance on regulations
  than results

You can communicate with them via email, instant message, Twitter®, Facebook®, LinkedIn®, texting or phone. They love technology.

In summary, this group is mature enough to handle important assignments and young enough to physically work more hours, even with sleep deprivation, than some of their more senior generation counterparts. Letting a member of this generation run a project with someone from the next generation working for him or her may be a match made for success!

Action Steps for More Effective Communication with Generation X:

• Do not micro-manage.

• Let them do it their way.

• Be flexible.

• Provide the latest technology in their workplace.

Generation Y

KIPPERS (Kids in Parents' Pockets Eroding Retirement Savings)
—texting shorthand from Generation Y

Members of Generation Y (GenYers) were born between 1981 and 1994 and are about 75 million strong. They are also known as "Trophy Kids" because they received a trophy for every team to which they belonged, whether they won or lost. The term "trophy child" was coined by psychologist Lee Hausner in her book *Children of Paradise,* published by Tarcher in 1990. Generation Y grew up with computer technology and understand it better than most members of previous generations.

GenYers have begun to believe what their parents always told them— that they are great. Their professors or employers may not agree. "Helicopter parents"—those parents who hover over their children—

have created needy children in some cases.

Having always had the latest technology, GenYers rely heavily on technology as a resource and a problem-solver. Before they were old enough to get jobs, they had their own mobile phones, which their parents gave them to keep them safe.

I recommend that parents of this group ease off and let their kids be more responsible for themselves so that they will be better equipped to succeed in the workplace. GenYers bring assets to an organization. They are optimistic about the future, are great at collective actions, have an unmatched ability to complete many tasks at once and are the most technologically savvy group. Use their "techno-savviness" to the organization's advantage.

GenYers appreciate organized, positive leaders who coach and mentor. They like working with other bright colleagues from their generation. Generation Y tends to expect excellence from others in their group. This is good to keep in mind in order to keep your good performers. This generation does not like leaders who use sarcasm or who treat them like youngsters.

GenYers can text faster than most people talk and prefer anything electronic. Provide the latest technology, and teach others to use it with them, or they will go elsewhere.

Action Steps for More Effective Communication with Generation Y:

• Be positive.

• Offer to mentor or coach them.

• Be organized.

• Have the latest technology available.

• Use technology to communicate.

Linksters

Linksters were born beginning in 1995 and are still coming. Today, they mostly work summer jobs. This group has always had technology and is even more savvy than Generation Y. Some say that, because they have always had computers, they lack social skills. They currently work entry-level positions and often interact a lot with customers.

Their idea of "appropriate" may be different from yours. Linksters often learn differently. Instead of giving them a manual, use interactive computer training or hands-on training with them.

Action Steps for More Effective Communication with Linksters:

• Be clear, direct and literal with assignments.

• Communicate electronically, yet encourage them to engage face-to-face.

• Teach interactively.

• Coach and mentor them.

Many organizations are on the brink of greatness and at the tipping point of success. We all want to be understood, and we can do so by first trying to understand others. Use some of these steps for better communication with different generations and watch your relationships, productivity, life purpose and bottom line skyrocket. You can definitely make your connections count across the ages!

BRUCE BRIGHT,
LtCol USMC (Ret), CCIM, CPC
The Bright Consulting Group, LLC

The guy to call when you want to LEAD

(205) 919-6829
bruce@ontargetleading.com
www.ontargetleading.com

Lieutenant Colonel Bruce Bright spent 28 years in the United States Marine Corps. His service includes 4 years as a Marine infantryman and 24 years as a carrier-qualified Marine F/A-18 fighter pilot. He logged more than 3,000 flight hours, commanded an F/A-18 fighter squadron and served two combat tours in the Middle East.

After retiring from the Marines, Bruce traded in his flight suit for a business suit. He joined the civilian workforce at The Sanders Trust, a privately owned real estate investment trust. In 2009 Bruce founded The Bright Consulting Group.

Bruce has a strong desire to help and encourage people using the experiences and lessons he learned in combat, in business and in life. He enjoys inspiring others with his motivational and inspirational speeches, life coaching, executive consulting and business training seminars. Bruce has a passion for helping people succeed and get what they want out of life. He delivers high-energy, humorous speeches on Communicating Between Generations, Supersonic Sales, Energetic Peak Performance; Convincing Customer Relationships and Being a Force for Good—Ethically, Morally and with Integrity.

An Unconditional Connector
Is an Influential Connector
By Ken Rochon

*I*n order to be an influential connector, you must decide to contribute to every connection you make. Fortunately, this is simple if you are willing to try something quite different than you may have been told or trained to do when networking.

In my experience, I have seen elevator pitches too many times. Practiced until it was so smooth it sang like a song that even Mohammed Ali would envy. Being an influential connector is not about how smooth your pitch is. It is not about how many business cards you collect during a networking event. It is not about the amount of connections you make on social sites. *It is about generating value for the connections you make through unconditional acts of contribution.*

When you meet someone, it might sound great to ask how you can help. What really counts is doing this action *within 24 hours* of meeting the new connection. This demonstrates to the new connection you are a serious connector, and it plants the seed early that you are influential.

It is important to have a system. Write your promise to connect him or her with someone on the person's business card, or record a reminder, or text that person right now. I prefer to send a text message to the other person and let that contact know I have a great connection for him or her.

This unconditional act of contribution to your new connection has created three synergistic moves.

1. You took action and that will be noticed as a sign you keep your promises and have integrity. Since the other person's experience of networking has possibly been empty and meaningless, you have shown you are different. You stand out!

2. If you have done a good job of matchmaking, you have created a win-win for both of your connections and this will not go unnoticed. In fact, they are probably already thinking of how they can return the favor.

3. Because you connected that person to someone you trust, he or she will have nothing but nice things to say about you. Thus, you do not have to toot your own horn. You have someone already eager to share how *influential* you are by giving you an endorsement that has an impact far greater than anything you could say about yourself.

Now, the power of your actions is clear. How do you contribute to another person? Let's begin with how you contribute to yourself and build from there.

Be a "Power-of-One" Problem Solver

I remember being attacked in broad daylight in front of an entrance to a park when I was traveling in a foreign country. I still look back and wish there had been someone there to help me. People with whom I shared the story asked me, "Did anyone help you?" I asked them if *they* would have helped me. This led me to ask myself the same question. There are so many opportunities to help others in this world, and many times we miss an opportunity.

Do not let the psychological phenomenon of the bystander effect stop you from being an unconditional Power-of-One connector. Maybe 99 out of 100 people would not connect others unconditionally—this does not mean they are correct. If you look at anyone who is successful, he or she did what the other 99 did not do. They did the exact opposite of what everyone else was doing.

The quickest way to be an influential Power-of-One connector is simply by looking for opportunities to make a positive difference. When I see a problem I either can solve or can help solve with the assistance of my network, I look at it as an opportunity. When you are known for being able to solve problems, you automatically have influence because you will likely be recommended to others as a problem solver. This is a great reputation to have.

Since you never know who someone knows, I encourage you to help anyone you have the power to help. You could be helping a child, and the parent finds out and recommends you for an opportunity. You may help a retired person and find out they are a potential investor in one of your projects.

I have experienced some amazing connections because I put myself out in the world as a Power-of-One problem solver. One act of promoting a man named "The Scary Guy" led me to meet many leaders in the Baltimore, Maryland, and Washington, DC areas. These connections eventually resulted in my being nominated to participate on a reality show called *Good Fellas of Baltimore*. When I received word I had been chosen, I could not help marveling about how this happened. It happened because I had invited the producer of this show to "The Scary Guy" event. He loved the message about acceptance, contribution and making a difference. This example of being a Power-of-One connector certainly made a difference in my life.

Assess Your Current Image and Message

You need to check yourself and make sure you are ready to play this big game of making a difference. My first recommendation is that you call in your top five advisors—the ones who care about your success. In order for you to be an influential connector, it will be important to hear what they have to say about where you are now. Ask questions like:

• How do I come across now?

• What do I need to work on?

• How is my image?

• How is my brand?

• How is my look?

These are critical starting points you must take seriously if you wish to be a master connector—someone who can make as many connections as you wish while keeping your promises to everyone.

What Do Your Business Cards Say About You?

What do your business cards convey about you? Do they complement your message and your mission? Do they let people know you have integrity and are a professional?

I have seen business cards that have mistakes and look as if the person is trying out this career. If it works out, he or she will get some real business cards.

You have only one chance to make the statement that you are committed to what you do. Everything has to complement that image and statement.

Although it may not seem important, you need to invest in your business cards. They make a statement about you in more ways than you can imagine. I work with several artists to make sure I have talented people designing my first impression. After all, a business card may be the only evidence someone has after an event to evaluate and remember you. Make sure your card is accurate, clean and makes a statement about the message you are trying to convey.

Once you have this stellar business card, get ready to feel abundant. I suggest you order 5,000 cards. Yes, this is probably five times more than you usually order. Not every connection you make will be one that turns you into an influential connector. However, if you go to a networking event and only bring enough cards to network with twenty percent of the folks there, you will be one-fifth of the influential connector you hope to be. I recommend you have 1,000 cards in a box in your vehicle, so you can go back for more if you run out during the event. For more on this subject, see Patty Farmer's chapter, *Getting the Most Out of Your Networking Organizations,* on page 109.

Give Two, Take Two

Make sure you give each person two cards, even though this may seem wasteful to you. However, I assure you the connection you are making is not going to give away his or her *only* card. You need to give that person an extra in hopes he or she will share your card. Of course, this is a reciprocal process. You also need to request two cards, so you can do your job connecting that person both at the event and after the event.

Learn what he or she is looking for and help find it. Do not make deals with people. It is not a situation where you do something for someone, and that person does something for you. Just prove your influence is from your heart. Be an unconditional contributor to someone's success and that will win you more points than anything else will.

Since you have a large collection of second cards, I suggest you put together a business card book you carry with you to refer these connections when you are out doing business. You also may store them electronically. However, there is something to be said for visible business cards. I remember being a deejay and having to remember where a song was located in a box of music. As I flipped through the CDs, I would find other solutions, and they would become templates in my mind for future searches.

Convert Offline to Online Connections

It is important to convert your new, offline connections to new, online ones. Find connections on Facebook®, LinkedIn®, PerfectNetworker.com®, Twitter® and other sites you use and learn who your new connections are as people. Discover your mutual connections and thank them for connecting with you. See *Networking in the Digital Age* by Sima Dahl on page 155 for more on online networking.

I suggest you have a daily regimen, at least a ten-minute "exercise" program when you communicate with your network. Show them you care about them. You can start by sharing an inspirational thought or quote or maybe some tasteful humor. Some members of your network will read it and others will comment, opening the door to connect with you more. *Social Capital,* Nanette Bosh's chapter that starts on page 165, has some great tips on this subject.

Wish a "Happy Birthday" to all the birthday folks that day. If it is a holiday like Father's Day, Mother's Day or Thanksgiving, I highly recommend you connect with as many people as you have time for and send them customized—by name—messages on those special days. Think about this: The average person may have 500 people in his or her network. If you are only one of 20 people who remembers to wish that person a "Happy Birthday" or special holiday wish, you stand out! Again, you are helping the seeds you have planted as an influential connector sprout bigger and bigger.

Before you retire for the evening, it is a good idea to see what posts you received while you were offline. In addition, a different section of your network is online at that time of day, and you have a chance to post something new that may catch *their* attention. For more information on when to connect with your network online, see *Twitter Strategies* by Gail Nott on page 175.

Convert Online to Offline Connections

Since friends of your connections will hear great things about you and want to connect, I encourage you to accept these connections— they are probably people who have heard you have great influence. Concentrate on making these online connections more real through engaged conversation that leads to phone calls, meetings and invitations to networking events.

Up to this point, I have shared with you how to create connections through simple acts of kindness. Because you have shown your agenda to be pure through your acts of unconditional contribution to your connections, your network will speak highly of you and will recommend you as a person they trust.

Now it is time to contribute to them personally and professionally through content. When you read a great blog, book or tip or see a movie that would make your network connections better, recommend it. Share great content with your network. Tag specific connections in messages to acknowledge their greatness.

We Are Influenced by Like-Minded Connections

Many social sites have groups you can join that allow you to interact with people who share common interests. Some sites take this a step further. For example, PerfectNetworker.com® has an Advanced Search feature, which allows members to connect with other members who share things, such as the same birthday, books and music. This is powerful because you can enter different aspects of yourself using these advanced search features and then quickly filter for people to whom you relate based on those characteristics. If you take a few minutes each day and farm for different aspects of yourself through these advanced search features, you will grow a connection base that is intrinsically linked to you.

It is important to utilize each site for its strengths because some social sites do not allow unlimited connections or do not allow you to connect with people you do not know.

Keep Your Eye on the Golden Prize

Sometimes, we run into people who do not "get it," and this may either disappoint or frustrate us. I suppose that if everyone "got it" then no one would be special. This is not unlike appreciating sunny days because the rainy days put things into perspective.

When you focus on unconditional connecting, you are, in essence, being an unconditional contributor. This is big!

Being unconditional means you are connecting with no strings attached, no agenda, no scoring. Once you let the person know what you did, you have changed the dynamic of the action and the relationship. That person will know you are someone who takes action to get things done. I cannot emphasize enough that this is *a code by which to live.* It does not matter if someone does not return the favor, referral or connection or does not even say "Thank you." This is not why you made the connection.

As an unconditional connector, you are on a pure path to make a difference. When you choose this path, the biggest difference you will make is with yourself. When you are truly living the life of an unconditional connector, you will experience peace in the true sense of the word. I always look forward to connecting people, and the difference I am making gives me purpose. I believe you can experience the same thing. The reward is in becoming so influential and successful that you will be overwhelmed with opportunity and joy.

ABC = Always Be Connecting

There is a reference to this with regard to the C equaling "closing" in a great movie called *Glengarry Glen Ross*. I treat "closing" as "connecting" because if you really connect, the closing will follow. It can follow for a long time if you are connecting with contribution.

Challenge yourself to connect with someone you do not know every chance you get. Whether you are at a gas station, the grocery store or waiting in line, smile and connect with someone. You may be amazed at how influential you can become if you connect with ten people a day. Ask for two business cards and hand out two of your own. Then invite people to connect with you online. Connect them with people in your network and watch the magic begin again and again.

If you consistently play the game of connecting and contributing to those with whom you meet, you may soon be considered an influential connector everyone wants to know. Happy networking!

KEN ROCHON
Perfect Networker

(443) 904.4545
ken@kenrochon.com
www.perfectnetworker.com

Ken Rochon has been an entrepreneur since 1989 and is just getting started! Today, he is a published author, world traveler, global fusion DJ for his company Absolute Entertainment, and co-host of *Team Radio*. He is a co-star of the reality TV show *Good Fellas of Baltimore* and the visionary builder and co-owner of Perfect Networker, as well as Perfect World Network—a community of charitable organizations. Ken was awarded *America's Most Influential Business Connector* in 2010 by the U.S. Small Business Conference.

Through his company, Perfect Networker, Ken has created a unique networking experience. It combines the human element with a virtual environment to provide its members with opportunities to share knowledge, ideas and referral business and to promote each other's success online and at face-to-face events. An elite team of multi-lingual ambassadors supports the members.

Perfect World Network is one of Ken's high-impact initiatives. It brings leaders of charitable organizations and non-profits together to connect and support each other in an online community. The excellent advantages of cross-promotion for events, benefits, fundraisers and memberships boost website traffic, increase members' teams of volunteers and much more!

To Strike Networking Gold,
Go on a Treasure Hunt!
By Betty Liedtke, CDC

When you know where to look and what to look for, you'll find golden opportunities to make valuable connections everywhere you go.

I don't do "networking" anymore. Instead, I go treasure hunting. That's because the most successful networking I have ever done, and the most valuable connections I have ever made, happened when I was not networking at all. I was having ordinary, everyday conversations with people at personal and professional events, and during casual encounters. In the process, I have discovered pure gold. That's why instead of networking, I now look for buried treasure wherever I go. I always find it—and you can too.

Put on your best swashbuckling shirt, grab the treasure map you will find later in this chapter, and set your sights on the next business or social event on your calendar. Once you start looking for buried treasure, you can find riches beyond your wildest dreams.

> *"You will get all you want in life if you help*
> *enough other people get what they want."*
> —Zig Ziglar, American author and motivational speaker

What Is "Buried Treasure?"

The kind of treasure I am talking about is any talent, trait, gift or skill that can be of value—financial or otherwise—to the person who possesses it. It is *buried* treasure if the person who has it does not recognize it, does not know or believe it has value or does not realize what it is truly worth. For example:

- A beautiful, powerful singing voice is an easily-recognized talent in a band's lead singer or in someone who performs regularly in musical theatre. However, that same talent can be buried treasure in a person who sings just for fun, or in the church choir. Look at the buried treasure that was discovered in April of 2009 when Susan Boyle appeared on the show, *Britain's Got Talent!* At age 47, she stunned the world with her singing.

- Many people who are organized make a living as professional organizers. The same skills can be buried treasure in someone who cannot stand seeing things out of place and always puts them in order or rearranges them for better efficiency.

- A flair for clever combinations of color and fabric can lead a person to a career as a designer. Someone who has a distinctive style and always looks terrific may have that same creative flair as buried treasure.

Please note that buried treasure is not determined by whether or not you are earning money from it or using it in your profession in some way. It is determined by whether or not you even realize that you have it or recognize its value.

How Can Someone Possess Buried Treasure and Not Even Know It?

The main reason people remain unaware of the treasure they possess is that their talent feels so common and ordinary, and comes so naturally to them, that they don't consider it to be anything special. If you call their attention to it, they are likely to shrug it off, saying, "Are you kidding? It's no big deal. Anyone can do this." Or perhaps they recognize their skill, yet underestimate the level or degree of their proficiency. They think, "If I can do this, anybody can do it," assuming and implying it's a universal trait, and other people just need to apply themselves a little more and they'll be able to do it just as easily.

Another reason people don't recognize their own buried treasure is that they don't see it as having any practical value. If it's not related to their education, training or background, or to the job they have or the career to which they aspire, it often goes unnoticed and unappreciated. This pertains to skills and talents, as well as to qualities and character traits such as compassion or determination.

I recently read a newspaper story about a couple who owned what the wife described as "an ugly vase." Her husband had had it since he was a child. When the couple mentioned the vase to an antiques appraiser at an annual Junk Bonanza Festival, they discovered that it was worth about $14,000.

Every few years or so, I read a story similar to this one. It typically involves a painting, dish or knickknack that someone sells for a few dollars in a garage sale or pawn shop and which turns out to be worth thousands—or even millions—of dollars. Everyone envies the shrewd or lucky buyer who discovered the item and made a fortune on it. However, I always find myself feeling sorry for the seller. He or she was in possession of a valuable treasure and didn't even know it. The item collected dust in the basement, attic or garage until someone else realized what it was worth and profited from it.

Unlike paintings, vases, jewels, coins or other physical objects that can be bought, sold, broken, lost or stolen, the buried treasure inside you can never be taken away. It is a part of you, and, with good fortune, you will always have it. However, it still won't do you any good or enrich you in any way if you don't recognize it or understand what it's worth. Like the couple who owned the "ugly vase," you'll be in possession of a valuable treasure and you won't even know it.

Finding That Buried Treasure

In my coaching practice, I help people find both their buried treasure and ways in which they can use it to enrich themselves and others. However, the purpose of this chapter is to help you find the buried treasure in *other* people. You strike networking gold by helping other people find their buried treasure, not by discovering your own. Let me be absolutely clear on this: you do this for *their* benefit, not your own. As you embark on this treasure hunt for networking gold, your purpose is to give, not to get. What you will discover in the process is that when you become a treasure hunter focused on helping other people discover and recognize their buried treasure, your own treasure chest will fill to overflowing with valuable riches and precious resources. Here's why:

- **Treasure hunters are memorable people.** When you notice and point out to people the talents, strengths and skills they don't even realize they have, you make a good impression on them in two ways. One is by opening their eyes to a valuable resource they did not realize they possessed. It cost them nothing to acquire it, and now that they're aware of it they can use it wisely and intentionally, and they can profit from it in different ways. The other reason you make a good impression is that even if you just met and spent only a few minutes talking, you obviously gave them your full and undivided attention and listened thoughtfully to whatever they said—enough so that you noticed and called attention to something about them that turned out to be a source of buried treasure. Since people want to do business with those they know, like and trust, they will likely remember your name because of your memorable encounter.

- **Recognizing the buried treasure in others helps you discover your own.** It is difficult to recognize and discern our own natural traits and talents, yet once we start noticing them in other people we can more easily identify those same traits—or similar ones—in ourselves. This relates to something I once read described as "the blue Honda® theory." Even if you have never owned a Honda or a blue car before, as soon as you buy a blue Honda, you'll start seeing them everywhere. It is as if every third person on the planet bought a blue Honda the same day you did. This is because something you never paid attention to before is now on your radar. You are now aware of it wherever and whenever you see it—even in yourself.

- **When you make others aware of their buried treasure, they will often do the same for you.** During a presentation a few years ago, I mentioned how much I admired people who were organized, especially since that's not one of my natural talents. I also made a joke of the fact that I file by tote bag. I collect tote bags and use a different one for each different project and program on which I am working, and for each of the different organizations to which I belong. When I'm on my way to a meeting, all I have to do is grab the right tote bag and be on my way. After the presentation that day, someone came up to me and said he thought I sounded very organized *and* extremely creative. He suggested I write a book about creative organizing techniques. He even suggested a clever title for the book. Whether or not I actually write that book someday—and

I probably will—I will *always* remember and appreciate the person who pointed out my buried treasure of being creatively organized!

- **Buried treasure grows and appreciates in value.** Suppose you give a friend or relative one of your possessions, such as a piece of jewelry, or a sum of money. Once that person has it, you no longer do. Now suppose that what you had given that person was some advice or information he or she needed, rather than a physical object. That person has it now, and so do you. You haven't lost it in the process of giving it to someone else. This is precisely what happens with buried treasure you discover and share. Your supply of it doesn't get diminished. Rather, it grows and expands, and the benefits it can provide you and others continue to multiply.

Following are three examples of people who discovered buried treasure in their lives. Their treasure was buried in different ways and for different reasons. Once they discovered it, they were able to use it to benefit and enrich themselves and others.

- Janet Roper is a modern-day Dr. Doolittle. Her company is Talk2theAnimals, and she helps owners of pets with training or behavioral issues. While talking with Janet at a networking luncheon, I found that she has always been able to communicate with animals. I asked her what it felt like to grow up with such an unusual talent. She said, "I didn't know it was unusual. I thought everybody could do it."

- Karen Bennett is a friend who is an avid and talented quilter. I am in awe of her ability to select and coordinate colors, textures and designs, and turn them into works of art. To me, the work she does looks like magic. However, whenever I admired her quilts and the talent it took to create them, she used to roll her eyes and say, "Betty,

I just cut out pieces of fabric and sew them together. That's all I do." The people, myself included, who are fortunate enough to own one of the quilts she has made—or who have seen the work she now displays in quilting shows and competitions—would beg to differ.

- Chez Raginiak is an author and motivational speaker whose story I first heard during a Toastmasters® speech contest. When I told him he should write a book about his experience of escaping from communist Poland in the 1980s and building a new life in America, he said, "I wouldn't feel right doing that. There are so many people who had a much more dangerous and difficult journey than I had. Besides, it would probably be so depressing that no one would want to read it." Today, his award-winning book of poems, *My Escape to Freedom,* serves as the inspiration for many of his speaking programs.

When you point out someone's buried treasure, they may not see it as such—at least not right away. That's not your concern. Do it anyway, then let it go. The universe has a way of bringing things full-circle, and that means that treasures and rewards will come back to you in unexpected ways, at unexpected times and places. This has happened to me many times, and I always enjoy hearing when it happens to others too. If you'd like to experience it for yourself, I suggest you set out on a treasure hunt of your own.

Use the following treasure map of tools, techniques and clues to help you discover and point out the buried treasure in other people. As you become more experienced at treasure hunting, add your own systems and procedures to this list. Then enjoy the satisfaction of helping others find unrecognized traits and talents. Watch how quickly your own riches and resources start piling up as you begin discovering buried treasure wherever you go.

Treasure Map for Networking Gold

1. Keep your treasure-hunting tools tuned up and in good working order. The best tools for treasure hunting are your eyes, your ears, your instincts and your curiosity. Although it's difficult to do in our fast-paced, sound-bite society, give people your undivided attention when you talk with them. That way you can see and hear what they do and say, as well as whatever may be just below the surface of their actions and words. *That's* where you'll find buried treasure.

2. Have your treasure-hunting equipment with you and turned on at all times. Your radar should always be turned on so you don't miss opportunities to discover buried treasure when you come across it. Pay attention at social and informal events, as well as at professional events or traditional networking opportunities. Do not turn into a stalker or predator. Simply train yourself to hear and respond to things people say and do that indicate a skill, trait or interest you recognize as potential buried treasure.

3. Look for patterns and hot spots. When people get more energetic, excited and animated about a certain topic of conversation, or when all roads seem to lead to the same subject or activity, you're in the vicinity of buried treasure. Keep digging, and you'll soon find it. By asking respectful and non-intrusive questions, you may discover a mother lode!

4. Share your own treasure with others. Be generous. This doesn't mean handing out your business card to everyone you meet. Nor does it mean giving out free samples or free medical, legal or computer repair advice if you are in those professions. It simply means giving freely of whatever you have or do from which others can benefit and that won't deplete any of your resources other than the time it takes to share it. Be quick to offer sincere praise, appreciation and compliments.

5. Remember the golden rule: no strings attached. To give something and expect something in return is standard and accepted behavior. Reciprocity is a powerful motivator. However, even more powerful is a gift offered with no hidden agenda or strings attached. If you can truly remove any hopes or expectations for yourself when you give others the gift of buried treasure, you will stand out from the crowd. You will be the person others remember, trust and treasure.

There is buried treasure in everyone. Take the time to find it and acknowledge it, and you will be amazed at everything you discover: golden opportunities, precious contacts and connections, and rich and rewarding personal and professional relationships.

Happy hunting!

BETTY LIEDTKE, CDC
Find Your Buried Treasure, LLC

(612) 743-1488
betty@findyourburiedtreasure.com
www.findyourburiedtreasure.com

Betty Liedtke helps people discover buried treasure—gifts and skills they don't even realize they have. What others consider to be ordinary traits and characteristics, Betty recognizes as valuable resources that can enrich their "owners" professionally, personally and financially.

Betty found her own buried treasure while digging through her life lessons and experiences—including developing breast cancer after her second child was born and severe heart damage from chemotherapy—for messages that could be of value to others. Her discoveries led to the founding of her company. Find Your Buried Treasure, LLC. Through writing, speaking, and individual and group coaching, Betty gives her readers, audiences and clients the tools to discover their own buried treasure, to achieve their dreams and goals, and to enrich themselves and the world.

Betty is a Certified Dream Coach® and Certified Dream Coach Group Leader/Spiritual Leader, and is one of forty female entrepreneurs from across the United States and Canada featured in the book, *Fearless Women, Fearless Wisdom,* published in 2010 by Fearless Women Publishing. Betty treasures the connections she makes as a member of Toastmasters® International, eWomenNetwork® Dream University® and in all her relationships.

Networking:
One Relationship at a Time
By Eleanor Parker, MBA

I woke up one morning in August 1996, and found myself living in Ridgetown, Ontario, Canada, a town of 3,300 people. Ridgetown is one community in a municipality of 110,000 people that includes seniors, men, women and children.

This was a small pond.

The only people I knew were my husband, my father-in-law and his significant other. This was vastly different than my previous pond— Southern California—where there are millions of fish in the pond.

The reality of my situation did not really make an impact on me until early 1999 because before that, I was busy adjusting to married life and a 12-year-old stepdaughter. In spring 1998, my precious son arrived, and I was busy adjusting to motherhood and an infant. I loved every minute of it. However, nine months later, I realized I could not be a stay-at-home mother. Then reality set in. How do I find a job without knowing anyone?

To find a job, I needed a network and I did not have one in this small pond. I started to make some phone calls and ask around for associations and networking events for business, professional and entrepreneurial women. I planned to start attending and making connections that would ultimately lead to a job. I soon learned the only organization was the local chamber of commerce. I had never relied on that organization for my networking activities before, and I did not want to start now. I was shocked to learn that nothing existed in this community where business women could gather to support and encourage each other, solve problems, and inspire and motivate each other to move forward with their goals, hopes and dreams.

Most people start a network to support an existing business—it is how they generate leads to grow their business. I had no business and decided that building a network would be my business. My vision was to build this network and hold regular lunch meetings where women could gather to meet and I would publish an annual directory of the membership. I started to "pound the pavement" to meet women and share my vision with them.

Some looked at me like I had just grown three heads on my shoulders. Others welcomed me and thought it was exciting and others wondered where I had come from with all this excitement and energy. In the end, I created a network. Today, ten years later, I am considered the networking specialist for business, professional and entrepreneurial women in the community.

The Art of the Cold Call

Creating and nurturing a network of contacts is the most effective strategy to build a business and drive revenues.

When I started to pound the pavement, every stop was a cold call. I did not have a warm, natural market. However, I did have a cold market that was not quite sure what to think of me.

At first, my names list was the phone book and the chamber of commerce directory. I preferred the chamber directory—it lists names, and then at least I knew the people I wanted to talk to.

Three Steps to Building a Great Network

Befriend the people you meet. I decided to take the time and resources to make cold calls my "friends." It is important to note that your friendship with these connections must be sincere, authentic and genuine. The reality is this: You will connect with some people and with others, you will not—and that is okay. In the long run, it made my life easier as these new friends started referring me to their contacts. Generally, people like to help other people. When my new friends learned I was new to the area, they wanted to help me and started to share their network with me—long before Facebook® came along.

Referrals from friends have many benefits:

• They tend to refer more often themselves, thus deepening your network.

• They tend to spend more money and spend it more often, therefore they become more valuable clients and customers.

• They are typically much more loyal and profitable, especially since there are no acquisition costs involved in getting them as clients.

I always had one goal in front of me—to turn a connection into a welcome with a warm handshake the next time I met someone. How did I do this? By engaging the person with whom I was meeting in a conversation about themselves.

People love to talk about themselves and I came prepared with questions to ask them. For example:

- How long have you been doing what you are doing?

- How did you get started in the business?

- What do you like best about what you do?

- What are your biggest challenges?

- What do you do when you aren't working?

If there are pictures of family in the office, I ask about family. Let me add here that I am someone who is genuinely interested in other people. Therefore, my interest in them and their lives comes from a sincere and authentic place.

Stay connected to contacts throughout the year. I send holiday cards, especially Thanksgiving cards, and cards for other occasions. If I know their birthdays, I send a birthday card. My goal is to connect with each person four times a year.

Go back on a consistent basis. The directory I published was renewed each year. For that reason, I called on all the network members once a year to renew their memberships. Each time I went back to visit them, they were anxious to see me—they wanted to fill me in on what had happened in their lives since I was there the previous year. In my first year of building my network, I called on the director for a national financial services company. Each year I went back, and each year the conversation would pick up where we had left off the year before! It became a running dialogue. One year, we discussed his son heading off to medical school; the next year, his recent big real estate purchase. The next year, we discussed his son's upcoming wedding; the next year, his medical school graduation and acceptance into residency. The year after that, the topic was his new grandson. This network friend has now become someone I meet with to brainstorm creative marketing ideas.

Relationships Matter . . . Connections Count

The reason for building a network is to transition you through life easier. How you connect with people on a human, personal level will ensure your success. Relationships are the key.

Years ago I met someone who would become a special mentor to me. He taught me the value of a relationship. He was the director of development for a major beer company and I asked him to support a fundraising event I was working on. No one had introduced us and he was a cold call for me. I just called him up one day and asked for fifteen minutes of his time. He agreed to give me just that and I went to our meeting prepared with my fifteen-minute presentation.

I was three minutes into my presentation when he interrupted me and asked me where I had gone to university. I was shocked at the question, and told him the name and that it was 2,000 miles away, near where I grew up. His next question shocked me even more—he asked me what my mother thought of my living so far away from home. I had never been asked that question in a business meeting by someone I had just met. We spent the next hour talking about university, family, life and my goals. I never did get to finish my presentation that I had so carefully prepared for this meeting. When it was all over, he gave me a big hug and told me that he would help me.

On my way home that night I realized what this man was doing— he was getting to know me. He received thousands of requests for assistance each year and they all wanted the same thing—beer and money. He always wanted to help everyone, so his strategy was to get to know the person sitting in front of him and that connection would determine his level of assistance. He taught me that it was not about the presentation or what I was asking for— it was about the connection and the relationship.

> *"Networking is not a numbers game. The idea is not to see how many people you can meet; the idea is to compile a list of people you can count on."*
> —Harvey MacKay, American author

The difference between living in a small pond and a big pond is this: Relationships matter more in a small pond. Each connection you make has the potential to be invaluable. When you live in a big pond, there are millions of fish from which to choose. You have a never-ending list of people on whom to call. A small pond has a limited number of people—every connection counts and every relationship matters.

Several years ago, I received a call from a lawyer who had received a magazine I was publishing for my network. She was calling simply to tell me what a beautiful magazine it was. Well, I jumped at the opportunity and invited her to lunch. After all, a lawyer who picks up the phone and calls someone just to give a compliment understands the human spirit.

We met for lunch, and for me, it was the beginning of a special friendship. As I got to know her, I came to value her wisdom and insight. We got together for lunch four times a year to chat about life, family, friends and work. After a few years, I stopped publishing the magazine because our family was going through a challenging time. My mother-in-law was dying of cancer and we were providing all her care. I just could not do it all. As a result, my lunches with my new lawyer friend stopped for a few years. However, I did stay in touch by sending her a card now and then. Those cards kept me connected to her. When I was ready to resurface, the connection was still there, and the relationship continued where we left off.

I am now embarking on a new journey with my network. I am taking it viral to support women with *big* ideas living in *small* communities.

When I did my preliminary launch for the founding membership for this viral network, my lawyer friend was the first one to call and tell me I had not included an address on my membership email. She wanted to be a part of this network and asked for a mailing address so she could send me the payment for the membership fee.

Much of networking advice is about having a network that includes members of various powerful and influential professions. We are advised to have a lawyer, a doctor, an accountant and so on in our network. In a small pond, there are only so many doctors, lawyers and accountants. If everyone building a network asked these professionals to be a part of their network, they would no longer have time for their own practices.

A more effective approach is to create a network that works for you and that is unique to you. Your network will:

• Help you deal with minor, daily challenges

• Help you find role models, mentors and advice when you need it

• Provide you with financial assistance, entertainment and someone to fix your flat tire

• Help you find a doctor, a mortgage specialist and a nursery school for your kids

Include someone who will let you cry on his or her shoulder when you have had a bad day, someone who will kick your butt and make sure you get right back up afterward, someone who will let you feel sorry for yourself—and someone who will not. Your network needs someone who will open a door for you at just the right time. It must include people who support, encourage and inspire you to be the best *you* you can be, to take risks, and to help you accomplish your goals, hopes and dreams.

Two years ago I was having a very overwhelming Christmas season. Everything seemed to be going wrong. I was trying to juggle way too much. It was December 23rd, and I was having a fit because I had no centerpiece for the table. I had run out of time to get it the day before, and now it was too late. My family was coming that day to celebrate Christmas. While I was feeling overwhelmed and inadequate because my family Christmas dinner table would not be perfect, the phone rang. It was one of my network friends calling to tell me how crazy her day was going. We compared stories. I am not sure whose was worse. However, two hours later, the local florist delivered a centerpiece for my Christmas dinner table with my family—courtesy of my network friend. She thought one phone call from her to the florist would change my day—and it did. It also showed me the beauty of the human spirit. That is why everyone needs a network.

Success Actions to Take

Make a list of everyone in your network. This list should include everyone you know—not just clients—and everyone who knows you and what you do.

Develop your PING strategy. Eighty percent of building and maintaining relationships is staying in touch. A "ping" is a quick, casual greeting. Put everyone on your list in one of three columns:

- Column A includes people with whom you are actively involved—friends or business associates.

- Column B is for the "touch-base" people in your life—casual acquaintances or people you know well.

- Column C includes people you do not know well or to whom you are not able to devote time.

Now, create a plan on how often you will connect with these people:

- Column A—monthly

- Column B—four times per year

- Column C—once a year

What else can you do to make your connections count? Here are more ideas:

- Think of three people you need to thank for something they did to make your life easier. Send them cards today and thank them.

- Did someone give you good service lately? Send a card to fifteen of your network friends and recommend this service to them.

- Send a card to two people whom you admire as role models and tell them why you admire them.

Why stay in touch with people in all areas of your life, both personal and professional? The answer is simple—to strengthen and deepen those relationships.

Why send a card and not just fire off a quick email? Because we are living in an impersonal world now and everyone is sending emails. A card received in snail mail will be remembered by the person who opens the envelope. Be memorable and intentional in your actions. Be sincere, authentic and genuine.

If you care about the people in your network and let them know you care, they will care about you—and will be there just when you need them. That is the magic of building a network.

Always remember—it's all about the relationship!

ELEANOR PARKER, MBA
Eleanor & Company

Relationships Matter . . .
Connections Count

(519) 674-2278
eleanor@eleanorandcompany.com
www.eleanorandcompany.com
www.sendoutcards.com/eleanorparker

Eleanor made networking her business when she moved from Southern California to Southwestern Ontario, Canada, and settled in a small community called Ridgetown. When she moved, she only knew a few people. Now, after networking extensively since 2001, Eleanor is considered the networking specialist and connector of people in her community.

Eleanor has experience growing a business in both a small community and a large urban center. This led to her passion for helping women in small communities make their hopes and dreams a reality. Her vision has expanded, and she is now building a viral network for business, professional and entrepreneurial women with big ideas living in small communities across Canada. Eleanor also started a marketing consulting practice to help professionals and small businesses nurture their relationships with their clients and incorporate referral-based strategies into their marketing program. For Eleanor, it's all about the relationship!

One of the reasons she became an entrepreneur was to enable her to schedule work around the needs of her young son. Her number one priority has always been—and remains—her family.

Great Givers Give Great Referrals
By Michelle R. Donovan

At some point in your childhood, a wise person—maybe your mom, dad, or grandparent—probably said to you, "If someone does something nice for you, you should do something nice for them." What that wise person didn't know at the time was he or she was teaching you one of the most powerful business lessons in history. Most people genuinely feel as if they need to do something in return after another person helps them in some way. That is the foundation of the Human Law of Reciprocity. In business today, you will make your best connections with people who live by this law of kindness.

Think about the times people helped you with your business. Maybe they referred you to new prospects, sent you hot tips related to your market or took you to events and introduced you to their friends. Maybe they promoted your event to their networks. How did you feel afterward? I suspect you felt really good about them. So good, in fact, that you felt compelled to reciprocate and help them in some way too! There you have it—the Human Law of Reciprocity in action!

How Do I Live the Concept of "Givers Gain®"?
Living with this mindset is truly living what my friend Dr. Ivan Misner, the father of modern networking and founder of BNI®, the world's largest networking organization, refers to as "Givers Gain,"

which means exactly that. The more you *give* in life, the more you will *gain.* The more you give in business, the more business you will gain!

When you take the Human Law of Reciprocity and make it a lifestyle within your business, you become much more proactive with your relationships. You begin to initiate the activity that actually ignites the reciprocity in others. You begin to actively look for ways to provide opportunities to others. You begin to focus on giving to others in everything you do. Your first thought upon meeting someone is no longer about what they can do for you. Instead, focus on what you can do for them. You begin to ask questions like "How can I help you?" "What support can I offer you?" "Who can I connect you to in my network to help your business?"

> *"The value of a man resides in what he gives and not in what he is capable of receiving."*
> —Albert Einstein, German-American physicist
> and Nobel Prize winner

How Does Focusing on This Law Bring *You* More Business?

Giving people become the center of their network. Other people are attracted to them. People want to be around people who are willing to help them. Their likeability factor goes through the roof!

When you position yourself at the center of your network, others will come to you for advice, resources, connections and help. The more other people come to you with their needs, the easier it is to give to them. The more you solve their problems, expand their network, provide them with resources and make connections for them, the more they feel the need to return the favor.

Before you know it, people start saying, "You've been so good to me. How can I help you?" At this point the opportunity for your network to refer you has never been greater. Hence, you stand to get new referred business—and lots of it.

A Referral is a Referral . . . Right?

Wrong. Referrals vary greatly in quality. Believe it or not, most people give the lowest quality referral. The sad thing is they never consider the impact on the quality of referrals that they would receive from others. What typically happens is that we get frustrated when the other person isn't giving us the kind of opportunities we want. It's quite simple—if you give junk, you'll receive junk. In other words, if you give low quality referrals, you'll also receive low quality referrals and therefore the stage is set. If you want to receive higher quality referrals you must first *give* higher quality referrals.

What does a higher quality referral look like and sound like? There are six different levels of quality with respect to referrals. Basically, the higher the quality, the more involved you are in the referral process. Typically, the more involved you are in the process on behalf of your colleague, the better it is for the person receiving the referral.

Level One: You give a name and contact information. This is the lowest level of referral and the most common. It involves nothing more than you passing a prospect's name and contact information to someone in your network for that person to call. Often, when the referred prospect receives a call, they have no idea why your colleague is contacting them. It's embarrassing and disappointing for your colleague. This is not much more than a glorified cold call. If your colleague gets past the gatekeeper, he or she still has a lot of work to do to close that sale.

Level Two: You give authorization to use your name. This elevates the referral slightly and insinuates that you have a relationship with the prospect. However, you still have little involvement in the referral process. Your colleague then calls the prospect with the high hopes that your name will pave the way. Why else would he use your good name if there wasn't some kind of connection, right? Unfortunately, the prospect responds to your colleague with, "John who?" Again, this is awkward for your colleague. If your relationship with the prospect is not strong and this happens, you really didn't do your colleague any favors.

Level Three: You promote your colleague in an introduction letter. At this level, you are more proactive and invest more of your time in the referral process. Once you've identified a prospect for someone, you craft a letter or email to that person introducing and promoting your colleague. You may even include some of your colleague's promotional material such as brochures, business card, website or one-page description as an attachment. Promoting your colleague is much more powerful than your colleague promoting him- or herself. In the latter case, he or she is selling—and most people don't appreciate being "sold." You, on the other hand, can gently open the door further by leveraging your relationship.

Level Four: You get permission for your colleague to call. At this level you are taking the referral one step further. Once you've done the work to promote your colleague, you simply ask "Would it be okay for my friend Clare to give you a call?" When the prospect says "Yes, have Clare call me," you now have permission to pass this person's name to your colleague, who now has a wide open door to someone who wants to talk to her. This level of referral walks your colleague right past the gatekeeper. More business will actually close because now he or she is dealing with someone who may want to buy, rather than someone who is just willing to listen to your sales pitch.

Level Five: You arrange a face-to-face meeting. Promoting people face to face is usually the fastest way to close a deal. Let's say you have a prospect for your colleague. This time, you're going to really raise the bar. At this level, you arrange for the three of you to get together to introduce the two of them face-to-face. For example, you might invite the prospect and your colleague to lunch or coffee to facilitate the meeting. This is your opportunity to edify your colleague and explain to the prospect why you feel your colleague is a perfect fit for his or her needs. Typically your colleague and the prospect will do most of the talking. Your role now is to observe your colleague in person interacting with a prospect. Pay attention to the words your colleague uses to discuss his or her value. You could use those words in future referral opportunities.

Level Six: Bring your colleague a closed deal. Have you ever received a phone call and heard, "Hi. I was talking to Patrick today and he told me about what you do. I'd like to work with you. Can you tell me what I need to do?" How sweet the sound of a closed deal! Notice that you really didn't have to *sell* anything at all.

Imagine doing that for your colleagues and the appreciation she or he would feel. At this level you've become so knowledgeable on how to talk about your colleague, and you speak with such conviction, that you actually sell the prospect on behalf of your colleague. In some cases you might even be able to help with preliminary paperwork that you can then forward to your colleague. When your colleague reaches out to this prospect, he or she knows that the selling has already been done. The prospect has already expressed interest and has begun the process of becoming a client.

In reviewing these six levels of referrals, ask yourself these questions:

1. What level of referral do I wish to receive from the people in my network?

2. What level of referral will I commit to giving to others from this point forward?

3. How much time do I want to spend chasing people who need to be "sold?" The lower the level of referral you receive, the more work you need to do to close the deal.

4. If you received higher quality referrals on a consistent basis, what would it do for your business?

Living the Giver's Lifestyle

We have become somewhat wired to think of ourselves first when it comes to our businesses. That is what makes us so protective of our trade secrets and so suspicious of our competitors. We are wary of being taken advantage of and distrustful of other people's intentions.

Making a personal commitment to adopt a giver's lifestyle in your business might feel like a total paradigm shift. It might even seem to go against what you believe will make you successful. It might sound like fingernails on a chalkboard.

However, a giver's lifestyle will make you more successful than you ever thought possible. If you truly believe in the Human Law of Reciprocity, what you give to your network will indeed come back to you ten-fold.

Five Life Actions to Take to Become a Great Giver

1. Give more than you expect to receive. Imagine you have a bank account. You must build up money in that account before you can withdrawal from it. The same is true with our relationships. We must invest in those relationships before we can expect or ask for anything in return.

2. Consciously think of others before yourself. The next time you go to a networking function, focus on how you can help the people there succeed instead of how they can become your clients. Most of the people in the room don't even know you, so why would they become your clients? Consider this event as an opportunity for you to connect people to the people you already know. There's a plethora of giving to be done at any networking event.

3. Give simply because you can, not because you must. I learned this lesson from my Nana as a little girl. She gave to her grandchildren even when she had very little to give. She once said to my mother, "I will give so long as I can." Great givers give with no hidden agenda. They help people because they truly enjoy doing it. They connect people because they know they will bring value to each other. Making a difference in people's lives gives them a natural high. Giving simply because you can is totally authentic and is the purest form of giving.

4. Give as you wish to receive. I am constantly teaching my clients how to lead in their relationships. Leading by example is one of the greatest ways to model your expectations. As mentioned, if you want higher quality referrals, you must model those expectations by giving higher quality referrals. If you want people to connect you to their network, you must actively connect them to your network. Reciprocity will be mimicked by your network. Knowing that, take the leadership role. In the long run, you won't be working as hard because your network will be referring people who are ready to buy from you.

5. Listen for opportunities to give. Consider yourself a proactive problem solver. Listen for people complaining about things in their life. "My furnace didn't kick on today." "I hate my neighborhood." "I get so frustrated when my CPA has to get an extension on my taxes." Every time someone complains you have an opportunity to help them solve their problem. Most likely, you know someone to whom you could refer them. If you respond by saying, "If I knew someone who could fix that right now, would you like to meet her?" you will almost always walk away with the experience of giving to both that person *and* the person you are referring.

Your Personal Call to Action
Many experts recognize that it takes twenty to thirty days to create a new habit. I'm asking you to make a personal commitment to yourself and to your network that you will become the kind of giver your mom always wanted you to become. This may involve changing some of your behaviors, opening your heart, and seeing more opportunities, and it may take some time.

Keep these words of wisdom in mind every day and make a point to think of your connections first. Print out the five actions of a great giver, and post them on your refrigerator or frame them on your wall. If you commit to these five actions every day, you will become a great giver. By becoming a great giver, you will enjoy the bounty that life will send your way.

Ask not what your network can give to you. Ask what you can give to your network.

MICHELLE R. DONOVAN
Referral Institute of Western PA

Creating Referrals For Life®

(724) 816-1760
michelle@referralinstitutepittsburgh.com
www.michellerdonovan.com

Michelle is a best-selling author and known in Pittsburgh as "The Referability Expert." She owns and operates the Referral Institute of Western Pennsylvania, specializing in helping entrepreneurs get more referrals for their businesses.

A prolific writer, Michelle has contributed to multiple editions of the *Training and Development Sourcebook* published by Human Resource Development Press. She writes a regular blog that relates life happenings to referral marketing, and she has also published over forty articles on networking and referral marketing in multiple publications. Michelle's first book, *The 29% Solution: 52 Weekly Networking Success Strategies,* co-authored with Dr. Ivan Misner, was recognized as one of the top thirty business books of 2009 and hit #3 on the *Wall Street Journal* Best-Selling Books list.

As a speaker, Michelle has presented at several national and local conferences. She is known for combining meaningful substance with real-life applications.

How to Be a Memorable Connector
Stand Out, Get Noticed and Grow Your Business
By Cathy Jennings

*E*very day, you are bombarded with thousands of messages. TV and radio, newspapers and magazines, billboards and store signs, emails and voicemails—it seems that everything and everyone is vying for your attention.

On the flip side, this means you and your business are constantly competing for people's attention as well. How can you set yourself apart from the multitude of professionals and companies people encounter daily?

I have seen networkers try everything from huge hats with enormous bows to bright, crazy cartoon ties, from overly generous cologne that takes your breath away to make-up that belongs in Cirque de Soleil®. These are all memorable. However, they may not make you want to do business with them.

The good news is that you do not have to be into weird props or wear crazy clothes to create a lasting impression. No stunts and no shticks are required. You can distinguish yourself as a thoughtful, engaging person whom people want to know and do business with by truly connecting with the other person—not as another card in a collection, but as an actual person.

> *"You can close more business in two months by becoming interested in other people than you can in two years by trying to get people interested in you."*
> —Dale Carnegie, American author,
> speaker and self-improvement expert

Three Ways to Become a More Memorable Networker

People want to feel appreciated, interesting and valued. They want to feel good. Making others feel better when they talk with you gives them a positive association and a favorable opinion of you because of how you made them feel.

The following is a list of little things you can do to make a big impact and be memorable.

1. Be a Conscious Communicator

We live in a distracted society. Everyone is busy. People are encouraged to multitask at every turn. Families, friends and co-workers expect us to be accessible 24 hours a day. We often talk with someone in person and take a call on our cell phones at the same time. We write emails while on conference calls. If you are like most people, this can make you less focused and less conscious of how you communicate with others.

With today's technology, it seems interpersonal communication skills are starting to suffer. Being more aware of how you communicate, as well as being more engaged when you do, will make you an exception to this trend.

Be able to clearly communicate who you are and what you do. People are going to ask for your name, your business and what you do. So why is it so many people are completely unprepared to answer these questions?

Part of the problem is trying to give witty thirty-second commercials and clever elevator pitches, instead of just being friendly and conversational. I appreciate a creative or humorous introduction as long as it communicates who someone is and what she does. Nonetheless, commercials and elevator pitches are not conversation to me. They focus on selling and sound bites.

Remember, you want to have a conversation with another human being, not recite the copy from a sales brochure or a mission statement from a website. Talk to the person in a relaxed, communicative way. Use words you would normally use in everyday conversation, not industry jargon or overinflated vocabulary. Help the person understand who you are and what you do.

Instead of a scripted or rehearsed introduction, aim for a succinct, benefits-driven response. Think about how you specifically benefit your clients or customers. Rather than saying, "I'm an accountant," try, "I help small businesses save money on their taxes." Instead of saying, "I'm a life coach," try, "I show women in mid-life how to reinvent themselves and rejuvenate their careers."

A memorable introduction does not have to be witty or funny. More importantly, it is succinct, to the point and easily understood—and said with confidence and a smile!

Give the gift of your full attention. Have you ever spoken with someone at an event and noticed their eyes roaming the room or noticed them frequently checking their phone and email messages? How did that make you feel?

Our minds are always racing with everything we have to do—calls to make, projects to finish, errands to run. No wonder people sometimes find it difficult to concentrate and focus.

Our brains actually work against us. According to Andrew Wolvin and Carolyn Gwynn Coakley in their book *Listening,* published in 1995 by McGraw-Hill, the human mind can take in information about five times faster than it can produce the words to convey information. When you are not talking, your mind has "time on its hands" because it is taking in information quickly and not slowing down to translate thoughts and words into speech. When this happens, there is a temptation to let your mind wander, so you have to train your brain to stay involved.

To actively engage yourself in a conversation, try the following:

• Turn off your phone and put it away.

• Make eye contact with the person speaking to you.

• Ask thoughtful questions.

• Clarify your understanding by repeating or restating what is being said.

Listening is an active process. It requires focus and concentration. The extra effort you put forth will make your conversation partners feel valued and interesting. In addition, because getting and keeping a person's full attention is so rare, offering yours ultimately makes you a much more memorable person.

Remember names—yes, you really *can* do this! Do you throw up your hands and declare, "I'm just no good at remembering names!" Remembering someone's name and using it in conversation is more than just good manners—it is good business!

Committing a person's name to memory and using it shows respect and makes them feel important and valued. In addition, it makes a fabulous impression when you use someone's name, especially if you just met or only met once before.

Why is it so difficult to remember names? Most people tend not to focus on names when being introduced because they are busy thinking about how they are going to introduce themselves and whether or not they have spinach in their teeth.

When it comes to remembering names, follow the old adage: "Use it or lose it."

When someone tells you her name, you improve your ability to remember it if you use it immediately. The next time someone introduces herself to you, do the following:

- Listen carefully to the person's name.

- Ask her to repeat it if you did not catch it the first time.

- Say her name immediately after hearing it. "Karen, nice to meet you."

- Read the name aloud if the person hands you a business card.

- Use the person's name naturally in conversation, "So, Karen, what do you do?"

- Say the person's name when leaving the conversation, "It was great talking with you, Karen."

2. Be a Conscientious Connector
A great way to be remembered is by being a connector. Become someone who puts thought and effort into how you interact with others and how you can help them. They will appreciate and value you for your efforts.

Be a conversation catalyst. You walk into a room full of strangers or perhaps attend an event where you know only a handful of people. Do you quietly wait for someone to approach you or do you fearlessly walk up to someone and introduce yourself?

If you are like most people, you dread talking to people you don't know very well. Keep in mind, most people feel the same discomfort as you, and they long for someone to rescue them. This is where you can save the day!

You do not have to be popular, extroverted or the life of the party to be a good conversationalist. Simply knowing a bit about the host or speaker and the purpose of the event automatically gives you a conversation starter.

Also, think of how you can offer value to those you meet. Do you have a book or article about small business loans you could recommend? Do you know of a helpful website for entrepreneurs you could share? Do you have a few tips in your area of expertise you could offer? For example, if it is tax time and you are an accountant, can you share information about new filing procedures, new ways to save, new deadlines and so on?

Taking time to prepare before you network only takes a few minutes. However, the benefits can be never-ending. Being confident, knowledgeable and ready to participate in conversations makes you stand far above the average networker. People remember you as the person who "had it together" at the event and who was interesting to talk to.

Take the first step to start a conversation, and you can take the pressure off everyone. You will move things forward and feel more confident and engaged. Your efforts will be remembered and appreciated by everyone you meet!

Roll out the welcome mat for newcomers. As a member of an organization or group—whether it is one that meets face-to-face or one that only interacts online—take the initiative to welcome new people to the group.

When you see a guest or new member enter a room, give him a friendly greeting. Show him around and offer a few details of what to expect from the meeting or group. Then, introduce him to a few of the folks you already know. Include some context about each person and share the name and some information about each one as well. This will alleviate any awkwardness or fear about being new or an outsider. In addition, it will help to expand everyone's network and enrich everyone's experience.

The same goes for online groups. When you notice someone new has joined the group, be the first to introduce yourself. Ask a bit about who the person is and what he does. Then, look for other members with some common points of interest and include them in the discussion.

Make strategic introductions for people in your network.
Networking advice often focuses on finding *new* contacts and *new* people to add to your network. However, a great way to be both visible and valuable to your existing network is to create connections between the existing members of your network.

Choose someone from your network. Think about what that person needs—customers, referrals, a vendor or service. Now, think with whom in your network would it be good for them to connect.

Next, through an email or online sites such as LinkedIn® or Facebook®, send a message to both stating your thoughts on why they should know each other. Be sure to include some information about each person, her business, specialty or expertise and something positive you have experienced or observed about each person. Then, encourage them to connect with one another.

Since most people rarely do this, you will be remembered as thoughtful, helpful and the go-to source for bringing people together.

3. Don't Fizzle on Follow-Up

Ok, admit it. You have a stack of business cards from other people on your desk, in your purse or in a drawer somewhere. We have all done it at one time or another—got busy, got distracted, procrastinated, did not know what to say or do next. Consequently, we did not follow up.

Maybe you found this secret stash of cards weeks or months later and thought, "How can I follow up now? It's been too long!" Into the trash they went.

Do not waste your time and energy on conversations only to toss the contact information into the trash. Instead, follow these tips for fabulous follow-up:

Be timely. Eighty percent of networkers do not follow up with the people they meet at events and organizations. Are you part of this statistic? Simply by sending a quick email or handwritten note or by making a brief phone call, you can be remembered as someone who actually *did* follow up.

Besides being out of the ordinary, following up in a timely manner— which means 24 to 48 hours after meeting someone—makes it more likely the person you are contacting will remember you and the conversation you had. We all tend to talk to many people and have multiple things going on at any given time. Therefore, the longer you wait to follow up, the more difficult it is to be remembered.

Be personable. When following up with someone, remind him how you know each another. You meet people in various settings and have numerous projects going on, so they may not always connect your name with the meeting. Make it easy for that person by mentioning where and when you last spoke and something about your conversation.

If you promised to send them something or to do something for them—such as make an introduction by email—be sure you do so. If you mentioned getting together for lunch soon, offer some dates, times and places to get it on the calendar. Sooner is always better than later.

Avoid "relationship death by automation." One of my all-time, most annoying pet peeves is when I meet someone at a networking event exchange cards, and then he automatically adds me to a mailing list or newsletter list without my permission.

There is something called "permission-based marketing" without which your messages are called "spam." Having someone's business card does *not* give you permission to market to that person and add him to your mailing list. Stand out in a good way by *not* automatically subscribing someone to your newsletter.

Instead, when you follow up, mention that you stay in touch with your contacts with a monthly newsletter. Include a link or copy of that newsletter for his review and provide instructions on how to subscribe.

Connect on social media sites after meeting in person. Many people have their social media account links on their business cards, brochures and websites these days. After meeting someone in person, be sure to connect online as well. This will enable you to keep up to date with her, and for you to update her on your status as well, in an easy and efficient way.

Create a personalized invitation to connect instead of using a generic template message, such as "I'd like to add you to my network." Also, provide some context as to how you might know one another, where you met or what you have in common. This shows that you put some thought and effort into making the connection. For more on this key subject, see *The Importance of Follow-Up and How to Delegate It* by Joanne Lang on page 121.

Going Forward

> *"I've learned that people will forget what you said, people will forget what you did, but people will never forget how you made them feel."*
> —Maya Angelou, American poet laureate and author

Being a memorable connector is not so much about what you do, it is how you make others feel. Turn off your cell phone and really listen to the other person. Focus on how you can help her in her business, not just on what you can get from this relationship. Remember, use the person's name in conversation and avoid using business cards as bookmarks by following up right away. If you implement these simple strategies, you will be remembered for your character, contributions and ability to make connections.

CATHY JENNINGS
No Pressure Networking™

Transform your everyday conversations into new clients, new opportunities and more magic in the marketplace

(717) 713-7255
cathy@nopressurenetworking.com
www.nopressurenetworking.com

Chief Conversation Starter™ Cathy Jennings is a self-described "situational extrovert." She understands many folks would rather "chew a wad of tin foil" than network. She teaches that effective and enjoyable networking is actually a skill anyone can learn. Cathy's entrepreneurial journey began when she was five years old and sold rocks to her neighborhood mail carrier. She returned to these roots in 2004 when she officially fled corporate life to start her own business.

Through her workshops, trainings and growing family of books and training tools, Cathy shares her No Pressure Networking™ message and guides others to connect with ease so they can enjoy thriving professional and personal lives. Known as a "Business Cupid" by clients who have seen her networking gifts in action, Cathy's lessons and tips for making the most of everyday conversations are changing lives and businesses for the better, one great conversation at a time.

Cathy enjoys hiking, traveling, hosting get-togethers with friends and savoring delicious ethnic foods from around the world. She and her husband live in Central Pennsylvania with their two crazy, loveable dogs.

Set Yourself Apart by Doing the Little Things

*How to Build Relationships that
Keep People Coming Back*

By Jenny Bywater

*H*ave you ever wondered what creates a relationship that keeps a customer returning to the same store?

When you think, "I need to buy toothpaste," what store do you think of to purchase that item?

When you think, "I need shoes, or pants, or a new dress," where will you shop?

If you offer products or services, wouldn't you like people to come to you first?

Essentially, this is what advertising is all about. When you advertise, you are creating awareness in people's minds of the products or services you offer. In the advertising industry, this is called being "on their ladder." Your goal is to have them call you *first* when they have a need for your product or service. You want to be on the top rung of their ladder—or at least the top three rungs. See *The Authentic Connection* by SherryLynn Wrenn and Sandra Fuentes on page 25 for more on this subject.

Let's look at how stores or other vendors get on *your* ladder.

If they are a small "niche" store, they advertise the specialty products they carry. They become an expert in their niche—and you remember them when you need what they offer. They step onto your ladder.

The big box stores use branding and advertising to get on your ladder. When stores like Walmart® or Target® carry a large variety of products, they advertise as the place to shop for everything, to get the "best price, best selection and best service."

If they are a direct seller or a service provider, they focus on high levels of customer service to get your attention, in addition to making sure they are a fit for what you are looking for.

My grandfather was in sales during the Depression years, and he had one of the largest sales organizations in the country for the product he sold. He brought hundreds of people into his organization who were willing to work. As a result, he was extremely successful. As a child growing up, I asked him how he was so successful. He replied that he based his business on three specific principles.

As I have developed my business over the last thirty years, I have incorporated these concepts into my business, and now I want to share them with you. Operating according to these principles will set you apart from your competition and will help you build relationships with people so they keep coming back to buy more.

Here is what Grandpa taught me:

1. Sales is King! In this, he meant he was proud of what he did because each sale he made contributed to the world. I remember him saying one day, "Do you realize that *everything* begins with a sale?" Consider this: After someone makes a sale, the order is placed. The company manufactures a product and reorders parts or materials from other companies, which in turn order materials from more companies. People are employed manufacturing all those products, which are shipped from warehouse to warehouse. You could say this involves "trains, planes and automobiles," or trucks and all the people involved in the processes. Of course, the sales person and his or her company employees all take part in processing the order and getting it delivered to you. Now, think of the people who work at the lunch places where these office workers buy their lunch, the UPS® driver or the mail carrier. As Grandpa said, "When you think of it, thousands of people could be involved in the sale of just one item!"

Be proud of your profession and the products or services you offer. Look at a sale as your contribution to the economy. Think of all the people you are putting to work as you make each sale. Let this help you have a positive attitude and put a smile on your face!

2. Sell the Sizzle! Grandpa said that you need to reach people emotionally and create desire. Have you ever pulled into a mall parking lot, got out of your car and smelled the aromas from the nearby steak house? Does your stomach rumble and your mouth water as you think, "Mmm, a steak sounds good."? When offering your products, set an intent to create *desire* for your product.

How do you do that? Grandpa said to focus on what your products or services will *do* for people, not the details of the products themselves. For example, when selling my products I could explain all the "stats" like the sizes, shapes, weight and finish. However, those details may bore you instead of resulting in an order. Instead, I could share with you testimonials about how my products have helped businesses grow. This might get your attention. By sharing how my products can benefit you, I sell the sizzle and you place an order!

You need to see how your products relate to your customers emotionally. The way to do this is to develop a repertoire of benefits you can share. As you share the benefits of your products, you create that "Mmm-sounds-good" response, *that* "I-want-that!" reaction in people, and they will decide to buy. What are some benefits you can offer? Does your product or service solve a problem they may have, make them look or feel better, make their home more pleasant or make life easier? Your goal is to create the "why" they want to buy from you. Why should they list with you? Why should they purchase insurance from you? Why should they hire you? Set yourself apart by selling the sizzle.

3. People do not care how much you know until they know how much you care—about them! Grandpa always told me that *people* are what it is all about. If your goal is to be of service to people, your business will thrive. Yes, you are hoping to create a sale as you meet people. However, if you are more concerned about meeting *their* needs rather than your own, they will likely remember and come back to you again and again. They may also send their friends to you.

> *"If you take care of the people, the money will take care of itself."*
> —Carl Doerfler, German businessperson and my grandfather

Your mission is to give extraordinary service. When you look at people as dollar signs, they feel that energy. They interpret your vibes and believe you only want to make a sale. When you genuinely look at your business as a way of giving service and benefiting others, they will feel that energy and be drawn to you. The trick is to build a relationship that draws them to you when they need your type of products. Remember the ladder? Your goal is to build a relationship that puts you on the top of the ladder for your type of product or service.

Some people think they are in the business of selling a product or service. That is true. However, whether you are in direct sales, party planning, a service industry or any other business, you are more in the business of selling yourself. Your goal is to build such a great relationship that when a customer goes to one of the box stores, they would never consider buying the products there that you offer. They would always come to you instead.

Your customers respond and relate to you when you:

• Are confident in the profession you have chosen

• Have a high-energy, positive attitude

• Believe you are offering a product or service that benefits your customers

• Smile and are of service

Seven Ways to Develop Relationships That Set You Apart
To implement the above principles, let's consider some simple, yet effective, things that you can do by saying "Thank you" with more than just words:

1. Put a thank-you sticker on their copy of the order. If you have a retail store or do home shows, place the stickers at your checkout area and put the sticker on the order in front of them. Say, "I want you to know I really appreciate your business. Thank you! I look forward to helping you again."

2. If you are involved in the actual packing of orders, put a thank-you sticker on the copy of the invoice they get with their order.

3. Put a "Thank-you-for-your-order" sticker on the top copy of customer invoices. You are thanking them in advance of actually paying you, and it gives them a warm feeling.

4. Send a thank-you postcard after you meet people. Let them know you appreciate them and look forward to helping them again. Send it separately from the order. This is very effective in building relationships. Do the "box stores" send them a thank-you note after shopping with them? This goes a long way in building loyalty for your relationship and may put you at the top of their ladder.

5. If you have had a meeting or interview with someone, send a thank-you card or postcard. Thank them for their time and show appreciation for their input into your discussion. This shows you were paying attention to them and want to work with them again.

6. When people order online, you do not have a chance to do most of the above. However, you can send a thank-you postcard that says, "Thank you for your online order!" People may not be expecting it, and it can *cement* your relationship and keep them coming back to you!

7. When you meet new people, ask for their business card or contact information and tell them you want to send them a gift. Then be sure to follow up and send them a card telling them it was a pleasure to meet them and include the gift—a bookmark, magnet or other easily mailed gift. They will remember your meeting and will be reminded of you each time they notice that gift.

Let the people you meet know you are interested in building a relationship with them. If you are a direct seller, in a party or show situation you can place "customer care cards" in guest folders. Draw their attention to it and say, *I am so excited to meet you tonight and to share our wonderful products with you. Included in your guest folder is a customer care card. I would appreciate you filling out this card so I can get to know you better and be of service to you tonight and in the future.* You can implement this tool with any kind of business. For example, restaurants often put customer comment cards at the cash register or in the folder containing your bill for the evening.

If you are not going to follow up and work to build this relationship, I suggest you do not even start, as you will be giving them an expectation of a relationship that you have no intention of building. I have been to hundreds of parties over the years, and shopped in innumerable stores and used lots of different service vendors, and I have only had three party plan sellers personally call me afterwards to see if there was anything else I needed! Chances are I needed more makeup or skin care after that first meeting. What if I liked the prepared food products or spices I purchased? I might want to order them again. Maybe I bought a children's book for my first grandchild. I may want to purchase more books for that child or future grandchildren. Perhaps I went to a candle or home decor party or store and gave them my information for their list, yet I did not purchase anything at the time. That does not necessarily mean I do not want to ever purchase a candle or home decor item. See Joanne Lang's chapter, *The Importance of Follow-Up and How to Delegate It* on page 121 for more on this subject.

Define What Makes You *You,* Then Implement the Appropriate Tools

If building your business is your goal, then building relationships and making your connections count need to be on the top of your list. The way to do that is to have systems in place. A good way to decide what you are going to do is to first analyze what is it that *you* offer your customers that sets you apart from everyone else?

- Have you become an expert in your field? Set up an email list and send regular newsletters and ideas sharing your expertise.

- When people shop from you, can they earn credits toward future gifts? Set up a preferred-customer program. Offer reward cards and mark-off circles or squares with each purchase. Include on the card the gift they earn when the card is full.

- Do you make special offers on a regular basis? Set up a keeping-in-touch program. Put your hostess or customer information into a database or on a spreadsheet. At the beginning of each month, send out twenty postcards offering a booking special or sales special. A few days later, call those twenty people. When they get the postcard, they may consider the idea, and when you call them, they may say yes. You can also send cards on their birthdays, anniversaries and so on. Offer discounts for ordering in the month of their birthday as your gift to them. Then follow up with a call.

- If you do home shows, when people host parties with you, do they receive benefits *after* the party? We call it a "Preferred Host Program." Set up a spreadsheet or file system to keep track of your hosts. Offer them specials for repeat bookings or repeat orders. You can even use this program to encourage them to do more to prepare for parties.

- Do you have a website or blog your customers and prospects can go to for useful information and perhaps to place orders? Update it regularly with fresh content.

- When someone joins your team, how do you get them trained? What kind of training and support do you provide? Create YouTube® trainings they can access. Host monthly conference calls or meetings.

- If people need your kind of product right away, do you have "cash-and-carry" items they can get immediately? Take advantage of company specials to build up your supply.

- Are referrals a key source of new business for you? Do you have a referral or affiliate program that rewards customers for sharing you with others? Put something in all of your customer/prospect communications about this program.

Once you formulate what makes you unique, put systems in place to make it easy to set yourself apart. As you understand what drives customers' decisions about the people with whom they do business, you can more effectively develop the systems and "little things" that will set you apart.

People have hundreds—if not thousands—of choices for everything they want to buy, whether it is a product or a service. When you make a great first impression, show you care and offer great products or services, you will be at the top of their ladder. Then when they need the product or service you offer, they will come to you! Review your marketing materials, emphasize what makes you different, apply Grandpa's principles to everything you do and build relationships that keep people coming back.

Jenny Bywater
The Booster

We provide the little things that make a BIG difference to your business

(800) 553-6692
jennybb@thebooster.com
www.thebooster.com

Jenny Bywater, known as "Jenny B," is the founder and CEO of The Booster, which she started in 1981. She saw a need for products to help those in the party plan and direct sales professions make more money in less time. Since then, she has helped more than one million consultants "boost" their businesses.

Jenny offers training on how to be more effective in all key areas of business and provides products to easily put those principles into action. The testimonials on her website rave about how her products and high-energy training have helped her clients at least double their sales and significantly increase their overall business success.

For thirty years, Jenny has been helping consultants' businesses thrive and grow. She has developed more than 3,000 eye-catching stickers, postcards, buttons and more that get customers to ask questions, attend parties and order. What sets Jenny apart? She really cares about the success of her customers. Her goal is to make you successful.

Getting the Most Out of Your Networking Organizations

By Patty Farmer

I recently flew to a business-to-business networking expo. At the airport, new, full-body security scanners were in place and nearly slowed the entire security process to a halt. While standing in line with 135 other people, instead of becoming angry and frustrated by the circumstances, I realized this was a great opportunity to connect with 135 people from every walk of life and occupation. I approached people in line and said, "Well, since we're all getting our bodies scanned, I thought we might as well get to know one another."

Does that sound like networking to you? It does to me. I spoke with and exchanged business cards with almost as many people in the airport line as I did at the expo where I purposely networked! Always remember, *every* place you are is an opportunity to network.

Some experts claim you should target those with whom you want to network. Others believe everyone is a potential customer, collaborator, or someone who knows someone who can help your business in some way.

I believe networking is not just about meeting people who can directly and quickly increase your income. It is much more. It includes meeting people who may know others who may become customers or resources for you and your network. Your network can include a diverse collection of people who could become collaborative or strategic partners, mentors, peers and people who give you ideas or support and more.

Effective networking requires listening. Focus on how you can help the person in front of you. Consider how you may be able to help someone he or she knows, or help someone you know by introducing them to this person. Networking is not about you and your current needs. Good networkers continuously keep their eyes and ears open for potential connections or future collaborations.

"Each person's life is lived as a series of conversations."
—Deborah Tannen, American author and professor of linguistics

Most people do most of their networking at group luncheons and events or through their local chambers of commerce. However, there are other places to network that are less familiar, yet equally productive. To get the most out of these groups, you need to do more than show up. You need to be present—and that is not always the same thing. Get involved, volunteer for a committee or serve in a leadership role. In essence, do not be an observer—be an active participant! Allow people to get to know you before you even have a conversation about doing business. Be interested in the other members of your organization, pay attention to what is going on and look for opportunities to connect with someone new every day.

Although there are a few rare individuals who network naturally and effortlessly, networking is typically a skill that must be learned. Most people do not recognize the need to learn how to successfully leverage their networking activities and connections. After all, what use is networking if not done efficiently and effectively—keeping the ultimate goal of well-leveraged connections with mutually beneficial outcomes and deep business relationships in mind?

Through networking you can:

• Meet new friends

• Meet people with skills you want to access or with whom you want to collaborate in a future venture

• Meet people who spark your creativity or bring fresh perspectives to current challenges

• Gain new clients

• Most importantly, have many opportunities to enrich others without thought of gain

True networking, at its core, is primarily about giving and not expecting anything in return. When you build solid and trusting relationships through networking, you gain tremendous feedback and growth you could not find anywhere. You also learn how to assist your fellow networkers in an atmosphere where people foster and encourage productive relationships and communication.

Some people network with the intent to make money and achieve financial goals. However, those who network with a pure heart and virtuous intentions aiming to meet people and give unselfishly are the ones who ultimately profit the most in both tangible and intangible ways. Networking without an agenda is the key to success!

"It is better to be prepared for an opportunity and not have one than to have an opportunity and not be prepared."
—Whitney M. Young Jr., American civil rights leader

In networking, everything begins with an introduction or what some refer to as the "elevator pitch." However, the real key to success is what is known as the "one-on-one."

The Elevator Pitch

In a networking group environment, you typically have an opportunity to do some type of thirty- to sixty-second "commercial"—your elevator pitch. This commercial is your opportunity to share what you do, the type of referral for which you are looking or a possible strategic partner to whom you would like to be introduced. This is not the time to sell. The elevator pitch was originally designed to answer the question, "What do you do?" The name came from the amount of time it takes you to ride an elevator and pitch what you do to someone else in the elevator. During your elevator pitch or commercial, be sure to share a little about why referring you creates a beneficial connection for everyone and what differentiates you from everyone else who does what you do. Remember, this is your opportunity to let people know who you are and how you and your company can help others. This is about *you.*

The Ten-Minute Presentation

In your ten-minute presentation, you can go into more depth about your products and services. Again, this is not the time to sell. It is your opportunity to share what you do and what makes your company unique. Take full advantage of this captive audience. This is also about *you* and *your company.*

The One-on-One Meeting

The next, and most powerful aspect of successful networking is the one-on-one meeting. My definition of a one-on-one meeting is an in-depth, follow-up meeting usually after initially connecting with someone. During the one-on-one meeting, the focus shifts from *you* to *us.* The question becomes, "How can we do business together?" This is a whole different mindset.

Setting up a one-on-one meeting correctly helps ensure the best outcome. Follow these simple, yet highly effective steps for the most successful one-on-one meetings imaginable!

Before the One-on-One Meeting

Set the stage for success. Confirm your appointment 48 to 72 hours in advance. I prefer to do this via email so I have a "read" receipt. Make sure the email shows the address and time you are meeting. I often include a link showing a map and driving directions.

Include the following questions in your confirmation email:

• What is an ideal referral or client for you?

• To whom are you looking for introductions?

• Who are a few good strategic partners for you?

At the end of the email, I provide the answers to the same three questions about my business.

Exchanging this information in advance grants you—and them—the time and opportunity to go through your databases prior to the meeting. Since I created and implemented this confirmation process, my one-on-one meetings have been more successful than I ever imagined!

Providing this information before the one-on-one meeting allows you to spend the bulk of your time getting to know each other on a personal basis. I suggest you ask yourself the following questions and look for answers while you meet.

• Is this someone with whom I would like to do business?

• Do his or her values and belief system align with mine?

• Is this someone to whom I would feel comfortable referring my friends and clients?

Dress appropriately. If the purpose of your meeting is to discuss business, dress to reflect your professionalism. If you are a doctor or in the medical profession, it may be appropriate to come to a meeting in your scrubs during normal work hours. On the other hand, if you are an interior designer, it probably is not appropriate to wear jeans and tennis shoes. In any situation, remember to practice good personal hygiene—and do not forget breath mints.

Be aware of time. If possible, have an agenda you both can follow to make sure both parties receive equal time to talk about your businesses. One-on-one meetings are *not* about selling. They are about finding common bonds and creating opportunities.

If your guest attempts to sell or recruit, he or she is saying, "My business is more important than yours." You are both there to represent your businesses and to see how you can do business together.

After the One-on-One Meeting

The final and most important aspect of the one-on-one meeting is follow-up. If you said you would facilitate an introduction or referral, make sure you do so within 48 hours, or you could lose credibility and waste everyone's time. Follow-up is key! For more on this subject, see Joanne Lang's chapter, *The Importance of Follow-Up and How to Delegate It* on page 121.

People do business with people they know, like and trust. A one-on-one meeting is the best opportunity for someone to get to know you as a person and to start building a trusting relationship that can lead to friendship, as well as referrals.

> *"Networking is just strategic socializing."*
> —Bev Brough, Australian networking coach

How to Maximize Your Success
at Your Next Networking Event

It is important to consider what kind of networking event you are going to attend. Is it a chamber event? Is it an industry-specific event, such as a real estate happy hour? Is it business-related, such as a sales event? Is it a social event, such as an office holiday party? All social events can become business-related if you ask suitable open-ended questions at the opportune time in an appropriate way. Know how each event works, see how it fits your strategic goals and maximize your success by being prepared.

Networking is about others, not just about you. Make yourself more approachable by smiling and dressing appropriately for the occasion. Wear a nametag—and always place it on your right side. When you shake hands, the eyes will follow the flow to your nametag. Plan on arriving early and staying late. That is when the most amount of networking is done.

Have a brief elevator pitch ready. That way you are prepared when someone asks you, "What do you do?" Make it short, yet interesting, so people will want to talk with you. Remember, it is about starting a conversation and not about selling. Listen to what he or she is saying, ask open-ended questions and try to learn more about the person. Find out what you have in common, either personally or professionally, in order to start building a relationship.

Always try to listen more than you talk. The idea here is to intrigue people with enough information that they want to know more—not to inundate them with your life story. Be open-minded, smile, have positive thoughts and a pleasant and communicative demeanor. People will see you are in a giving mindset.

Avoid giving people the impression you are waiting for a pause to start pitching your business. Lean in and listen. Ask questions. Identify the person's needs. This shows you are receptive and it differentiates you from your competition. When you follow up afterward, you may be able to help by providing possible solutions.

Have plenty of business cards and treat them like gold. In other words, do not just work the room and wait for someone to pause and then hand over your business card. Wait until you are having a conversation and that person asks you for your card. This increases your odds of having someone keep your card and possibly follow up with you. See *An Unconditional Connector Is an Influential Connector* by Ken Rochon on page 47 for more on using business cards effectively.

When you receive someone's card, take a moment to look at it and make a positive comment about it. For example, you may like the design, graphics or colors. Always look at the card and then refer to that person by name. Say something like, "John, I really like the layout of your card, and the graphics really make a statement." This can go a long way toward building that relationship. It also helps you remember someone's name and to address him or her by name later. If the person asks for it, present one of your cards. Remember, business card collecting is not the same thing as networking.

Do not try to work the room by limiting yourself to a small amount of time with each person. Nothing is more obvious than when you are having a conversation with someone and he or she keeps looking at the time, as if gauging how much time is worth spending on you. If you are attending a two-hour networking event and there are 75 to 100 people present, you cannot speak to everyone. Again, be prepared and have a goal before you go to the event. Always aim for quality versus quantity when networking!

Trying to make contact or follow up with someone whose business card you obtained without some conversation is only slightly better than cold calling if you have no recollection of the person or business. While this approach does not guarantee failure, it certainly reduces your possibilities of success.

Calculate Your ROI *and* Your ROR

What do you consider your return on investment (ROI)? Networking is about relationships. People do business with people— and specifically people they know, like and trust. Some business professionals are the most concerned with their ROI. When you join a networking group or organization, it is important to calculate just what you consider your ROI, given that you are sometimes making a significant investment of time and money with any particular organization.

Even more important than ROI when networking is your return on relationships (ROR). Take your eyes off yourself and give without expecting anything in return—you will be amazed what networking can do for your business. When you shift your mindset and focus on the long-term benefits of your ROR, you will truly be able to make your connections count.

Evaluate your ROI—and your ROR—by answering these questions:

• What new skills did I learn or acquire?

• Did I have the opportunity to make changes in my business by learning what was not working?

• Did I receive discounts on products or services from other members in my networking group?

• Did I form new friendships and find new partners that enabled me to collaborate on projects?

- Did I collaborate on any joint ventures with someone who was a member, or someone I met through a member?

- Did I receive referrals that resulted in new client business and an increased bottom line?

- Did I receive referrals or introductions to strategic partners that resulted in a source of further referrals?

Networking is a powerful tool for any business and one that needs to be learned, fostered and integrated into your daily life. Become a master networker and watch your business flourish!

PATTY FARMER
The Networking CEO™

(972) 603-8209
patty@pattyfarmer.com
www.pattyfarmer.com

Patty Farmer, "The Networking CEO", is a highly sought-after public speaker, radio show host, author and marketing professional. Recipient of 2010's Best Business Connector in Dallas award and an America's Most Influential Business Connector nominee, Patty has created a network of close to 50,000 connections while teaching thousands of business owners how to network using a noncompetitive and dynamic collaboration strategy. Patty is the owner and director of the Texas Hot Pink Mamas, a professional business networking organization, and the founder of DFW Biz Link, a unique online-based networking, marketing and collaboration program for entrepreneurs.

Patty's first international venture is Biz Link Global. Offering pre-screened connections and collaborative partnerships, Biz Link Global enables business owners to expand their marketing endeavors worldwide through exclusive online tools and an unparalleled referral system. For this work she received the 2011 International Women's Day Service Award for Business.

In an age where so many are distracted by technological bells and whistles, Patty Farmer is a shining example of how passionate leadership, coupled with a truly personal touch can create a meaningful and enduring platform, bringing real-world and lasting benefits.

The Importance of Follow-Up and How to Delegate It

By Joanne Lang

I have always felt that focusing on building a relationship with a potential client was more important than focusing on the sale. People buy from you because they like and trust you, because they feel appreciated. Larry Page, co-founder of Google®, once said, "If you are not trusted, you have no business."

Following up is an important strategy for building relationships, cultivating trust and building a business. Many people underestimate the power of follow-up. Have you ever received a message from a potential client, answered his or her questions and waited for a call back that never happened? Would you have stayed top of mind or been more highly valued by that potential client if you had made a follow-up call or sent an email? The answer is yes. Never again let business slip away by failing to follow up.

Why Follow Up?

It is all about feeling appreciated. Diane Helbig, a professional coach, posted an article for *Small Business Trends,* May 2, 2010, about a study conducted by Dan Kennedy, internationally recognized as the "Millionaire Maker," to discover why clients leave their vendors. The findings were dramatic. Diane wrote, "Sixty-eight percent of clients who leave do so *because they feel unappreciated, unimportant and taken for granted."* The italics are mine because I want you to pay attention to this: You lose clients because they do not feel appreciated, and you can show your appreciation by following up appropriately.

Take care of your clients. Incorporate customer appreciation into everything you do—in every communication you send to a customer, in every interaction you or your staff has with each customer. In this way, you become known for providing high level customer care and it becomes an integral part of your brand.

Diane also wrote, "When I do sales training, I spend a significant amount of time on the idea that the prospect wants to know that you desire to do business with them—not just everyone. They want to feel valued even at that stage. As you navigate this prospecting stage, you do yourself a favor by consistently connecting with your prospect."

The contacts you meet at networking events need to be treated this way too. As you meet prospective clients, focus on them before you talk about yourself. Take time to write down some of the key points you learned for future reference. Talk about their family, friends, business and affiliations. Find out what you have in common. By jotting this information down on the prospect's business card, you can enter it into your database later. This communicates that you value them enough to learn about them and their business.

How often have you been to a networking event, made a connection with someone and never followed up? What happened? I assume nothing happened—unless that person followed up with you. Did he or she feel appreciated? Did you leave a lasting impression? Most likely, your name and face left the person's mind by day's end.

A contact is just a name if you choose not to follow up. When you do follow up, that contact is more likely to become a client, a referral source or both.

> *"Marketing today is dramatically different.*
> *It's no longer just market share and how much you can sell.*
> *It's also owning the customer relationship."*
> —John Sculley, American businessman and
> former CEO of Pepsi-Cola Co® and Apple®

No Time for Follow-Up?

You are not alone. Occasionally, many people drop the ball with follow-up. As a business owner, you are busy juggling your time between your prospects, clients and family. Finding time to follow up is a challenge. Could you be exploring potential business or are you missing opportunities because you are not finding the time for follow-up?

I encourage you to delegate follow-up to an employee or a virtual assistant. By delegating your follow-up tasks, you have a greater chance of winning your prospects over than if you make no effort at all. See my chapter "Growing Your Virtual Team" in *Incredible Business,* published by THRIVE Publishing™ in 2010. The individual to whom you delegate this project needs to understand that this is an extremely vital project. He or she must feel your passion for following up with your clients and know that this is the most important part of your business. Either your assistant will make a lasting impression, and the prospect will remember you and your business in a positive light, or will quickly forget you because your assistant failed to follow up.

Choose the Right Person

Here are seven steps to help ensure the person you choose for your follow-up will do it the way you want:

1. Get a referral from another business owner.

2. Ask your local chamber of commerce for referrals.

3. When you advertise, obtain a resume and a cover letter to see the candidate's communication style. Are there spelling or grammar errors?

4. Get four references from people with whom the candidate has worked and call them. Learn the person's strengths and weaknesses.

5. Notice if and how your candidate follows up with you. Did you receive a thank you note or other follow-up asking if you have made your decision?

6. Find out if the candidate has experience in selling and following up with prospects. What is his or her attitude toward the importance of follow-up?

7. Make sure the candidate will be compatible with your needs and the needs of your team. Will the candidate remain flexible in times of differences? Will the candidate be able to adjust his or her schedule for you? These are very important attributes to consider.

8. Give the person you choose small projects to begin with to gain your trust. Does this person meet deadlines, complete projects the way you want and communicate well? Once you are 100 percent satisfied he or she will do a great job, it is time to hand over the all-important follow-up project.

Make Sure Your Assistant is Successful

Ensure your assistant will accomplish your follow-up project successfully by using these six tools:

1. A system. Explain your system so your assistant can work with it.

2. An up-to-date database. If your database is not up-to-date, have your assistant complete this task first.

3. A phone script. The script is significant. It needs to be engaging and personable. The potential prospect needs to hear sincerity and enthusiasm in your assistant's voice. You want to make sure this conversation will make a positive impact on the prospect.

4. A phone with good clarity. Ensure your assistant will use a phone with a solid, clear connection.

5. An email script. This way your assistant will be sending a pre-approved email, and you can feel confident about what your prospects are receiving.

6. A card script. Whether you send a computer-generated card or write your own cards, give your assistant the script for that as well.

Have a Follow-Up System in Place

When you have a follow-up system in place, you can increase your sales and set yourself apart from your competition.

> *"The key to follow-up is to have a system.*
> *What is your follow-up system?"*
> —Eric Lofholm, American master sales trainer

Going to a networking event and walking away with business cards of contacts who could be potential clients is the first step. What's next? If you are like most, your office is laden with stacks of business cards wrapped in rubber bands awaiting your attention. I advise you to enter the contacts in your database and toss the business cards.

Find a Database Program and Keep It Updated

Find database software that will meet your needs, such as: Act.com®, which offers a free trial, SalesForce.com®, Microsoft Access®, Outlook® and Gmail®, which is free and has many beneficial tools. You can also use scanning tools, like the popular Cardscan.com® or Shape Services®, which has an application that scans the card right into an iPhone®.

When your database is updated, it is time to enter or scan the latest information into your database or delegate this task. Make sure you or the person inputting the data for you captures all of the information: name, address, email address, phone number, license numbers, taglines, where and when you met the person, the service in which he or she was interested and any additional information you discussed.

Your Follow-Up Note

Once all the information is entered, it is time to send a follow-up note. This can be completed with an email, a card or a letter. This note is only about the contact, whether they are a prospect or a potential center of influence. It is not a sales letter. In the note, build on the conversation you had when you met. Timing is critical here. Ideally, send the note the day you met your contact. This will make an impact on the person and help you stay top of mind. Of course, life is not always perfect. The maximum amount of time to complete this task should be within the week of meeting your contact.

If you find you are not getting your follow-up note out promptly, I recommend you delegate it. Your assistant can write the card for you or send an email on your behalf. If you do nothing, you lose the prospect.

I personally prefer email because it is faster. If I am asking a question or inviting someone to meet, it is easier for the person to reply to an email. State your purpose or personalize your comment in the subject line of your email. This will increase the chance that your recipient will read it.

I also enjoy using computer-generated cards that are sent through the mail, like Send Out Cards®, because you can include elements such as a photo of yourself, your staff and your office. People are more likely to hold onto a card with a picture than one without. This is a fast, effective way to connect, and it prints in your own handwriting, even though it is created on the computer.

Handwritten cards or letters are nice as well, and stand out among the stacks of mail people receive. This is a nice touch. People do not send them very often and the recipient definitely appreciates the gesture.

At the bottom of the note, I like to add a "by-the-way" clause. Here, you can explain a service you provide in which they may be interested. Here is an example, "By the way, I provide a monthly e-newsletter that gives you tips and techniques for growing your business. Would you like to receive it?" Some business owners like to use this clause to ask for referrals.

Stay in Touch

You cannot possibly follow up with all the people you meet on a regular basis. However, if you are in sales, you likely have more time to devote to your contacts. If you have a service-related business, follow-up activities can pull you away from your work and income.

For this reason, I really like e-newsletters to stay in touch. They keep me connected with everyone on a regular basis, and people enjoy receiving them. Make sure to offer relevant, up-to-date business tips oriented toward your reader and target market. I believe that the e-newsletter is powerful and one of the best marketing tools you can have. Through the service you use for your e-newsletter, you can generate autoresponders that will go out on a schedule consistent with your marketing plan.

Social media is another wonderful way to stay in touch. I have developed many relationships on Facebook®, LinkedIn® and Twitter®. You can provide valuable information, establish connections and develop relationships. Never oversell. The rule is eighty percent information and twenty percent selling. If your interest is just to sell, it is my feeling that placing an ad on the social media sites would be more appropriate.

Whichever way you choose to follow up with your prospective clients, it is important to get their permission first. I am a firm believer in permission-based marketing—99.9 percent of the time, people say yes. Your contact will appreciate you asked, and you will leave a great impression.

Schedule Periodic Meetings

Meet your prospect for coffee, or if you are located in different cities, meet via a video conference. Set aside one day a week where you only meet with your prospects. If you do this consistently, you can serve them more effectively. Build your relationships with your clients and prospective clients as you interact with them and get to know them on a personal level. This benefits both of you.

Ask questions of your prospect to find out if he or she would be an ideal client for you. Find out if the person is someone to whom you can refer your clients. Discover the best way to work together for each other's benefit. Again, this is not about the sale.

Other Ways to Follow Up

Throughout your business relationship, it is also nice to give your contact something of value. Now that you know your contact and what interests him or her, you can send blog posts, articles or emails that might be of interest. Your contact will appreciate the attention and the information you share.

A great way to network, exchange ideas and information, and get to know one another is to get a small group of your contacts together—ideally in person, although a conference call can work too. During your conversations, you will know if they are interested in your services. They will ask you questions and show interest in what you do. Find out when they would like you to follow up. Since this is a meeting to get to know one another, the selling happens later. Set the date on your calendar to follow up and then move forward.

Whichever method you use, it is important to focus on your contact and the great topics you discussed. John Jantsch, in the April 9th, 2010 posting on his *Duct Tape Marketing* blog, wrote that follow-up is a mindset that must pervade every process and touch every constituent group in your business. He believes that consistent communication by virtue of relevant follow-up is more of a way of life than a tactic.

An effective follow-up system is imperative. Remember, your prospects want to work with a business that offers excellent customer service and is one they can trust. What better way to show you are a person of integrity than by following up within a timely, consistent and professional manner. Before you know it, they will be glad to refer you to many of their clients. For more about following up, see Patty Farmer's chapter, *Getting the Most out of Your Networking Organizations* on page 109.

How can you improve your follow-up? Think of three things you can do right now to follow up and set yourself apart from your competition. Make your connections count with great follow-up!

JOANNE LANG
The Personal Assistant

Helping you bring in the business by providing marketing assistance and support

(916) 716-5800
joanne@thepersonalassistant.com
www.thepersonalassistant.com

Joanne founded The Personal Assistant in 2004 to provide experienced administrative services and support to entrepreneurs, executives and busy professionals. She gained strong organizational, time management and communication skills through more than twenty years of experience as an executive administrative assistant, licensed insurance agent and notary public.

The clients of The Personal Assistant include small business owners from zero to five employees. Though the team can help with all types of businesses, they have special knowledge in the financial planning, health and life insurance, public speaking, estate planning and real estate industries.

Joanne's passion is to help take her clients' businesses to the next level by providing marketing assistance and administrative support without the overhead of in-house staff. She specializes in coordinating speaking engagements, business-to-business marketing and seminar assistance. The Personal Assistant is one of Roseville, California's, most sought-after business resources. Joanne is also a co-author of *Incredible Business,* published by THRIVE Publishing™ in 2010.

How to Attract More Clients Through Effective Networking
By PJ Van Hulle

Networking is a great way to build your business. However, you may have spent lots of time, energy and money on networking events without getting the results you want. Whether you are clueless when it comes to networking or you are already a "networking ninja," this chapter will help you take everything to the next level.

Here is just a taste of what you will learn:

- The top three keys to super-charging your networking results

- How to determine which networking events are a fit for you and which ones are a waste of your time and money

- Five simple steps to prepare for a networking event, making every event go so much better for you

- My step-by-step system for how to follow up after a networking event

What Is Networking and What Are Networking Events?
A social network is a structure made up of individuals connected by one or more specific types of interdependency, such as friendship, family kinship or shared interests. A social network is a map of all

of the relevant connections between the individual people in it. A networking event is a chance to build, develop and strengthen that network.

There are many different types of networking events and groups, such as:

- One-person-per-profession referral groups like Business Network International® (BNI)

- Open groups like chambers of commerce —not limited to one per profession

- Women's groups like eWomenNetwork®

- Service and charitable organizations like Rotary International®

- Online social networking sites like Twitter®

- Business seminars like Client Attraction Intensive

- Trade groups like the National Association of Realtors®

You can experience great synergy by belonging to two or three different groups, becoming the networking bee that cross pollinates those groups by bringing referrals from one group to the other. However, I have found that belonging to more than three groups can be counter-productive. Attending too many events in a single week can cause exhaustion without the results to show for it. You may get so busy meeting new people that you cannot follow up and nurture those relationships.

How do you determine which events and groups are most appropriate for you and which ones are a waste of your time and money? First, find out how much it costs to participate in the group. Often, the higher the entry fee, the higher the quality of the networking. People who pay more tend to be more committed. I discovered one of the best places for me to network was a user's conference for a $300-per-month software product.

More importantly, find out if your potential clients or strategic alliances will be at that event or in that group. For example, it would benefit a mortgage broker to attend a local Association of Realtors meeting because real estate agents and mortgage brokers can make good strategic alliances.

The Top Three Keys to Super-Charging Your Networking Results

Key #1: Network for strategic alliances, not for clients. A strategic alliance is someone who serves the same niche or target market as you do, yet does not directly compete with you. Some people also refer to strategic alliances as referral partners or power partners.

Why is this strategic alliance focus so important? If you are focusing on enrolling one new client at a time, you are not leveraging your relationships—or your time—well. The average person has 250 people in his or her sphere of influence. Would you rather be looking for only one potential client or for someone who can bring you 250 potential clients?

Networking is not about closing a quick sale or meeting as many new people as possible. It is about developing meaningful relationships which lead to future business. Focus on making a few solid connections. When you meet someone who clicks with you, look for ways you can contribute to that person, whether you do business together or not.

When you network coming from a mindset of service and giving—rather than scarcity and taking—you will stand out and people will remember you. Over time, this method brings in more clients and more success.

You do not need a large number of strategic alliances to have a thriving business. I have managed to build several businesses to over six figures with only one or two key strategic alliances. In fact, a networking expert I know says that when you have just *seven* good strategic alliances, you will have more business than you will ever need.

Key #2: Prepare. The second key is to take the time to set yourself up for success before a networking event. This can make a world of difference. Here are five simple steps to preparing for a networking event:

1. Schedule time to follow up after the event—before it even begins. Most people leave a networking event with the intention of following up—then dive right back into their work day, pushing aside the critical step of following up in a timely manner. If you schedule the time in advance for follow-up, you are more likely to actually do it. For more on this, see *The Importance of Follow-Up and How to Delegate It* by Joanne Lang on page 121.

2. Refer to a packing checklist to ensure you have everything you need. Your packing checklist should be a document in your computer that you can easily locate that lists everything you may need for your networking events, such as:

- Plenty of business cards

- Sign-up sheets for a free giveaway

- A clipboard

- Flyers, brochures or media kits

- A raffle or drawing prize

With this checklist, even if you are getting ready in a hurry, you do not have to worry about forgetting something important.

3. Practice your response to the question "What do you do?"
When someone asks you this question, you have a fabulous marketing opportunity! Avoid saying, "I am a _____." People will automatically associate you with every other person they have met in your profession, assuming they know who you are and what you do. Instead, focus on solving a *specific problem* for a *specific group* of people.

When you do this, the other person will automatically start to search his or her mental filing cabinet for people who belong to that group and have that problem. Now you are much more likely to get a referral out of the conversation.

Does focusing on a specific group limit you? When you try to be all things to all people, you end up being nothing to anyone. Choosing a specific group of people to work with allows you to become an expert in that particular area. Then you can target your marketing specifically to that group—which is far more effective—and find them easily through your networking efforts.

Think about easily identifiable labels like moms, real estate agents or single women in their forties. When you ask someone, "Who do you know who is a real estate agent?" faces will probably immediately pop into their mind.

You may resist choosing a specific group because you are afraid you will limit yourself—and therefore your business growth. However, you actually limit yourself by trying to be all things to all people. The right clients for you will find it easier to differentiate you from your competition.

Just because someone is not exactly in your niche does not mean you cannot still help that person. One of the most life-changing workshops I ever attended was for holistic practitioners. They did not turn me away just because I was a real estate investor at the time, and I became one of their best clients.

Attracting new clients is like playing darts—your specific group is the bull's eye. Even if you do not hit the bull's eye, you still get points for hitting other parts of the dart board.

Is it negative to focus on a specific problem? The truth is that people tend to pay more for a cure than for prevention, and will avoid pain before seeking pleasure.

If the problem is painful enough, your clients will find a way to pay for the solution regardless of the economy. Imagine that you have just walked outside to your car to drive somewhere and notice that all four tires are flat and need to be replaced. You will find a way to make that happen, won't you?

Focus on solving a specific problem for a specific group of people and watch what happens. I have seen companies have their best year ever in a down economy just because they did this one thing well.

For example, I might say, "I work with coaches, consultants and speakers who are having the challenge of not being able to find enough clients who will pay them what they are worth."

Here are some more examples:

"I work with people with cerebral palsy to get function back in their limbs without pain." This man used to say "I am a Quantum Touch® practitioner."

"I support people who have tumors to heal them naturally without surgery." This woman used to say "I sell essential oils."

Test this template out for yourself. "I work with [insert specific group] who are having the challenge of [insert specific problem]."

See if you get a different reaction at your next networking event. If someone asks you, "How do you do that?" it is time to get excited because that means you have found an engaging response to the question, "What do you do?"

4. Practice your response to "How do you do that?" My favorite response to this question is, "There are lots of different ways I work with people, depending on what they specifically want. Why? Do you have someone in mind who might be curious about my services?"

5. Practice your infomercial if you will be giving one. An infomercial is a short presentation, usually thirty to sixty seconds long, that you give about yourself and your services in front of a group. Prepare your infomercial for success by including:

• A hook

• A message

• One specific call to action

• Your name

• A tagline (optional)

A good infomercial starts with a hook—something to get the group engaged. It could be as simple as inviting everyone in the group to take in a deep breath or raise their hands. Next, add the body or "meat" of the infomercial and a clear call to action like "Pass me your business card," or "Write your name and email address on this sign-up sheet." Finally, you can add your name and a compelling tagline like "If you do not take care of your body, where else are you going to live?" A tagline is not essential. However, it can help people remember you more.

If you have thirty seconds to give your infomercial, that is only six sentences for all of these elements, so keep them brief.

Key #3: Follow up! As mentioned earlier, implementing this third key to your networking success will be much easier if you schedule time *before* the networking event to follow up *afterward*. Also, it is important to follow up within 24 to 48 hours of when you met that person. After that, they may have trouble remembering who you are.

According to copywriting and marketing expert Vrinda Normand, only three percent of the people in any given niche market are actively looking and ready to buy your service at a specific time. Thirty percent will never do business with you simply because they are not the right clients for you or do not need what you offer. The other sixty-seven percent either do not know they need your service yet or are not ready to purchase at this time. When you follow up, you dramatically increase your results because you capture more of that sixty-seven percent who you would have otherwise left on the table.

Here is my step-by-step system for following up after a networking event:

1. Organize contacts.

2. Enter contacts information in database. Note: do *not* send someone your email newsletter or marketing materials unless they

have specifically opted-in to your mailing list.

3. Send a follow-up email.

4. Send a follow-up card.

5. Send friend requests on Facebook®.

6. Call hot leads and potential strategic alliances.

It helps to have pre-written generic messages for the follow-up email and card that you can adapt so you do not have to waste time starting from scratch after each event.

If you have a contact relationship management system (CRM) like Constant Contact®, 1Shopping Cart®, or Infusionsoft®, you can set up an automated follow-up sequence of heartfelt—not sales— messages, full of useful information. Save the sales pitch for later.

Send Out Cards® at www.sendoutcards.com is a great service for follow-up cards. You select or create a greeting card online and type in an address and message. The company prints a real card, puts it in an envelope, seals it, addresses it, stamps it, and mails it for you. You can even create a custom font from your own handwriting, upload pictures, and send gift cards, checks or packages with your cards. The system will even remind you when one of your contacts has a birthday or anniversary coming up.

I love Facebook for staying in touch and developing relationships. Here is the five-minute-per-day Facebook plan I recommend: set an alarm for five minutes, send out friend requests to the people you just met, read your friends' status updates, comment where appropriate, and when the alarm goes off, update your status. That's it!

Remember the top three keys to super-charging your networking results: network for strategic alliances—not for clients, prepare and follow up. You will be surprised at how many more clients you can attract through your networking efforts by implementing these three keys.

PJ Van Hulle
Real Prosperity, Inc.

Live your life out of freedom and joy instead of debt and obligation

(707) 718-6402
pj@realprosperityinc.com
www.realprosperityinc.com

Starting with $10,000 of her own money, PJ Van Hulle acquired over $6 million in real estate and created a six-figure seminar company. She was on track to be able to retire by the time she was 31.

When the real estate market crashed, everything changed. Her credit was ruined, she lost her home to foreclosure and she was forced to declare bankruptcy. After seeing her empire crumble, PJ realized that *making* money and *keeping* money were two entirely different skill sets. By helping other people avoid the financial challenges she had experienced, PJ turned her company around and doubled her sales. She is now passionate about providing people with the financial education to grow their money and keep more of it. Her dynamic, interactive and "plain English" style of teaching has helped hundreds of people to improve their relationships with money.

PJ is a certified trainer with thirteen years of teaching experience. She leads seminars, workshops and retreats on financial education, prosperity consciousness and how to attract more clients. Access PJ's free Networking Success Tool Kit at www.networkingsuccesstoolkit. com. PJ is the author of the *Little Book of Prosperity* published by Our Little Books® in 2011.

The Art of Connecting People
Five Steps to a Successful Networking Event
By Anne Garland, ASID

*I*n this fast-paced world of social media, I am still a bit old-fashioned. I believe face-to-face and one-to-one marketing is the best way to connect. It has the most impact and leaves a lasting impression.

Like online dating, you can only converse online for so long using email. Eventually, you have to meet in person if you are serious about making a connection. This usually is the turning point—either the beginning or the end of the connection—depending on how you handle it.

I have been connecting people for years by creating successful networking events—and you can too. Anyone can duplicate my skills with a few basic steps.

Creating your own networking events can be fun and profitable, and you will be in control and the star of the show! People will remember you—and isn't that the goal? We all know the value of connections. Here is a fresh perspective on making them count.

> *"One is the loneliest number that you'll ever do*
> *Two can be as bad as one*
> *It's the loneliest number since the number one."*
> —Three Dog Night, American '70s rock band

I do not believe this! I believe that when two people get together it is a party!

Everybody knows at least two people. Each of those people knows at least two people and so on. This is where your networking connections begin: A party of two can grow to a party of a hundred or more.

Webster's New World Dictionary Second College Edition defines *party* many ways. However my favorite definition is: "A group (number of persons) meeting together socially to accomplish a task." A task is the goal or end result. Every event planned has a goal or an objective, whether it is a birthday party, a corporate event for your entire sales force or coffee for two.

Here are the five steps to a successful networking event:

1. What Is Your Objective?

> *"An archer cannot hit the bull's eye*
> *if he doesn't know where the target is."*
> —Author Unknown

Plan with the end in mind. Why do you want to make connections and bring people together? Is your goal to sell a product? We are all selling something. Even doctors and hospitals are selling their services, and they too are competitive.

Are you planning to have a speaker motivate or train your guests? Maybe you want a panel of experts to exchange ideas or solve problems. All of this is your *why* for having people attend your event. It is the message you want to present to them so they remember you as the connector—which leads us to the second step.

2. What's in It for Them?

"Day, n. - A period of 24 hours, mostly misspent."
—Ambrose Bierce, American editorialist,
journalist and short story writer

You now know what you want. What do your potential contacts want? Why would people take time out of their busy schedules, leave their families and maybe pay money to share time with you? What is the value you will bring into their lives that would make them willing to spend time and money to join you? Put yourself in their shoes. There are only so many hours in a day, and everyone is pulled in a thousand directions. You need to offer a program packed with interest.

Will it be a program for a specific target market or will it be broader in scope to meet the needs of the masses? Knowing the answer to this is critical as it will help you define the size of your gathering, the type of location you want to consider and your basic theme. Will you need a quiet space or a more social setting? I have held small gatherings of ten where I used the conference room in the newest hip restaurant in a city, and it became very intimate. Everyone had a chance to get to know each other and walked away feeling satisfied with time well spent and meaningful contacts.

Conversely, I have had blowout events where, for example, I rented the ice skating rink at Rockefeller Center with a famous restaurant overlooking the rink. I brought in a few musicians and had a memorable evening with 300 of my closest friends. It was a new experience for most of the attendees—many of whom had lived in New York City for years. They could not wait for the next event and hoped they would be on the "A" list for future invites.

Tip: Go for the best venue your budget will allow since your goal is to impress them with the experience—which leads us to our third step.

3. It's All in the Details!

> *"Nothing can cure the soul but the senses just as nothing can cure the senses but the soul."*
> —Oscar Wilde, Irish writer and poet

This is where magic is made. One area that can really set you apart from the pack is the details. This is where all of the senses come into play, starting with sight—the visual appeal of the food, the surroundings, the table settings and the views from the windows. It includes how lighting is set, brightly or dimly depending on the mood you want to create in the space, the time of day and the audience. The subtleties of the environment have an effect on how a person feels. You can control this. The environment makes the same first impression as if you were meeting someone for the first time. Do not underestimate its power.

Consider how you feel when entering a corporate boardroom versus the dining area of your favorite restaurant. As an experienced interior designer, I understand the effects an environment can have on a person's mood. Consider this as you attend your next event. What emotion does the space evoke in you?

Let's venture into food. Taste is important and will be the most scrutinized factor of the event. If people do not like the food, it is downhill from there. It will not matter how great the speaker is or any of the other details—all your guests will remember is the bad food. Recently, I attended a long-anticipated seminar with one of the best speakers I had ever heard. Before his presentation, we spent time networking. There was a light fare of hors d'oeuvres and vegetable nibbles on the buffet table. It looked as if the facility food staff had forgotten to plan and had to send out for food at the last minute to a big box store and purchased frozen quiches and pizzas. It was awful! As much as I liked the presentation, what stands out most in my mind is the poor food. Thank goodness the wine was good! The moral of this story is: Know the venue's service and food before you commit to using their space. Do not leave it to chance.

When I worked in a large architectural office, we had weekly "lunch-and-learn" events where industry suppliers came in and gave a presentation on their products and services. This was a great example of networking. It was a win-win for the supplier and for us since we were often too busy to leave the office to have lunch. We also became familiar with new products. Thus, the term "lunch-and-learn." We tended to judge the supplier by the food he or she presented. If we liked the food, we were more likely to invite the presenter back, and of course we were more likely to specify their products.

Do not forget sounds in a room and check out acoustics and music for your space. Are you using live music or none at all? Will the size of the group and the space require amplification for the speaker? I sometimes find a microphone can be overbearing and less intimate. However, make certain everyone can hear the presentation. Will adjoining rooms be noisy and distracting?

Another one of the senses often overlooked is aroma. I suggest you consider this. An Italian restaurant creates very different odors than a Chinese restaurant. If you are considering an intimate space, you might enhance the room with flowers or fragrant candles, which will create a different feeling. Often, a special aroma can trigger a pleasant or unpleasant experience or memory for a person. For instance, think of apples baking in the oven. Doesn't that conjure a pleasant thought of a time when your mother made an apple pie that just melted in your mouth? How does that make you feel at this moment? Now, imagine hard-boiled eggs that you are cooking and preparing for an egg salad sandwich. A very different emotion surfaces. Any of these considerations can set the mood for a connection, depending on the desired effect, your event objective and the people involved.

When it comes to addressing the senses, the bottom line is to provide your guests with a distinct set of experiences. This is the single most important aspect of the event where you tie it all together, using the various senses as mood enhancers or mood changers, no matter how small or how big your gathering. With a little sensitivity in planning, paying attention to their sensory experiences will keep your guests interested and involved, even in the most subtle of ways.

Your event *must* be interactive. Create a way for everyone to get involved. Allow for an exchange among your guests and speakers so they get to know each other, or you may lose them. They may never realize why they feel blasé about the presentation or your event.

Here is a format I find works great for networking presentations with a group fewer than thirty. Ask each person to introduce himself or herself by name and location. Have guests briefly state what they do. I also ask them to offer either a comment on what they hope to get out of the presentation or a question they hope will be addressed based on their interests. You can have a marker board available and note each person's question on the board with the name notated. This lets them know that you are actively interested in them personally regarding their needs. At the end of the presentation, go back to each question listed on the board and make certain you have addressed everyone's needs or expectations. This is an amazing tool that adds value to everyone's experience and can help them feel a connection to you, to the speaker and to each other—which leads us to step four.

4. What Is the "Take Away"?

*"The intense happiness of our union is derived in a high degree
from the perfect freedom with which we each follow
and declare our own impressions."*
—T.S. Eliot, American-born English poet,
playwright, and literary critic

What were your guest's final impressions? Did you satisfy their needs and interests? Did you meet your objective? Was your branding message delivered?

Your real job as a facilitator or networking host is to *inspire* the audience. The speakers and the details of your production should create an enriching experience. What will they remember most about the time they have shared with you? Ask for feedback for the efforts you have put forward. I suggest you have a simple questionnaire for them to complete right before they leave to measure your success and their happiness. You are asking them, "How did I do?"

Before I share a sample questionnaire, here are a few guidelines:

• Keep it simple and easy with no more than five questions.

• If it is a conference, seminar or workshop, I suggest you use an onsite questionnaire to get their response before they leave. This is the best time to get the most honest response on the event. If you wait to get it later, they might not remember the details. You can offer a free lunch as an incentive for taking time to fill out the form and randomly select one of the finished questionnaires, similar to a raffle. Play with this and have fun.

• If it is a large social event, you should contact them afterward by email or regular mail. However, expect the percentage of responses to be reduced. They may not remember or maybe too busy to respond.

Here are some sample questions to consider. For the first three questions, ask them to respond on a scale of five to one from *strongly agree* at five to *strongly disagree* at one:

• I received valuable information.

• My expectations were met.

• What is the most significant message you received?

• What other topics would you like to receive in the future?

• Would you recommend us/me to a colleague? (circle) Yes No

• I am interested in attending more events (circle) Yes No

• Name, company, email address, phone number

With this type of questionnaire, you acquire updated contact information on your attendee. You might discover two or three strong candidates with whom you want to set another appointment to present additional information on your product or services. Isn't this the goal? This information can be invaluable.

This leads us to the final step—probably the single most important step—for you in making your connections count.

5. Show Me the Money!

> *"Success is not a destination, it's a journey."*
> —Zig Ziglar, American author and motivational speaker

Each of these steps has led you to the most important point—your connections. The planning and execution of the event has been the vehicle to reach the bulls-eye. I hope you have fun throughout this process. If you have fun, your guests will have fun.

The after-event marketing, or what some event planners call the *post-mortem,* is more than just evaluating your event and questionnaires or writing a thank you or even making phone calls—all of which are essential for establishing your brand. More importantly, you have established an invaluable database of fans who, if you have given them an unforgettable experience, may return to your next event *and* share it with their friends. This not only builds brand loyalty, it also builds more connections and business.

Networking plus connections equals money. It is all about making the right connections to meet the right people who will help your business grow. I have found that creative events and diverse programs have been invaluable tools to meet people who have led me to other people and so on.

It is true that the most effective and memorable events, no matter how small, are "shows." You, as the producer, must take responsibility for the details to produce a good "show."

With some creativity and proper planning, you too can create successful networking events that generate great results. Use the steps in this chapter to create a successful networking event. Determine your objectives, focus on the details and ensure an enriching experience for your audience to make your connections count through this medium. Here's to your success in the art of connecting people through networking events!

ANNE GARLAND, ASID
Anne Garland Enterprises, LLC

Always expect the unexpected

(860) 575-4970
anneg@annegarlandenterprises.com
www.annegarlandenterprises.com

Anne—pronounced *Annie*—Garland is the creative director and founder of The Idea Circle for Women, a division of Anne Garland Enterprises, LLC. She produces enriching, entertaining experiences that provide fabulous women an opportunity to grow together in meaningful ways.

Combining her sales and marketing experience with her expertise as a registered interior designer in Connecticut, Anne spent fifteen years with BASF® and Honeywell®—both Fortune 100 companies. She worked with creative and talented architects and designers to market products through her unique and creative style. She became known for her not-to-be-missed, educational, fun and inspirational events. Anne adapts effortlessly in today's fast-paced world by staying on top of issues that are most important to women in their 50s, 60s and beyond. She is a known as a "pollinator," or connector, and delivers amazing events focused on networking and connecting people to people.

An active member of the American Society of Interior Designers (ASID), Anne is a past president of the Connecticut chapter and has held advisory council positions on the national board. She is active in many networking organizations.

Networking in the Digital Age
The Brand Is You
By Sima Dahl, MBA

Networking has long been an important skill for career success. Professional associations, Rotary Clubs® and even Meetups serve to bring busy professionals together to network and learn from one another. In fact, according to its website, Rotary International® boasts more than 1.22 million members worldwide. That's impressive, right? However, consider this: There are a reported 940 million people using online social networks, 72 percent of whom regularly use two or more. Clearly the rules of networking have changed. If you want to make your connections really count, you must first accept responsibility for your personal brand—then engage in meaningful online networking to create champions for your brand.

"Starting today you are a brand."
— Tom Peters, American author and management guru

The Age of Referrals
While social networks have forever altered the way we relate to one another, the golden rule of generating referrals remains unchanged: People buy from people they know, like and trust. The same holds true for recommending job candidates and making referrals. The more we know, like and trust someone, the more we are willing to go to bat for them.

Growing up, my mom used to say, "It's not what you know, but who you know." In the Age of Referral, it is no longer who you know. Rather, it is *who thinks they know you.* My, how times have changed. I can get to Kevin Bacon in six hops and I know you can too.

Think about it. The better I know you, or believe that I know you, the more comfortable I am passing along your name, taking your sales call or recommending you for a job. The goal of purposeful social networking then is to create an army of personal brand champions who know you and know what you need. When done properly, social networking can help you build a network that instinctively acts on your behalf and in your best interests. That is what I call "sway." Here is how to use networking to develop effective sway:

1. Be the Brand

Your personal brand is simply this—who you are, what you do and why you are special. It is equal parts competence, character and charisma. Your personal brand is uniquely yours and helps you stand out from the pack of competitors. For example, it is no longer enough to simply say that you are a lawyer. A Google® search for *lawyer* returns roughly 77,200,000 results in less than 0.24 seconds. What kind of law do you practice? Who are your representative clients? What geographical area do you serve? These details help the members of your network position you in their mental Rolodex®.

As part of their training, my clients all write out their personal positioning statement. To write yours, follow these guidelines:

• **Keep it simple.** Convey your general expertise in plain English— avoid lingo.

• **Make it short.** Use as few words as possible. Aim for a few sentences that you can speak aloud in thirty seconds or so.

- **Be intriguing.** Why are you unique? Come up with a hook. "I own a chain of laundromats" does not hold a candle to "I created New York's first chain of eco-friendly laundromats that cater to urban professionals with free Wi-Fi, phone charging stations and 24/7 espresso carts."

- **Aim for excitement.** Being passionate helps make you memorable. If you are not excited about who you are, how can you expect anyone else to be?

I encourage you to share your written draft with a couple of close members of your network to get their honest feedback. Once you are satisfied that your written statement accurately captures your unique positioning, create a second version that you can easily say when you meet in person, chat by phone or video chat via Skype®.

2. Practice Your Pitch

Once your personal brand statement is ready to go, practice delivering it in front of a mirror. Then practice it some more. This is particularly important for anyone going through a career transition. If you are out of work or switching career paths, your pitch should reflect the position you ultimately want to achieve.

I learned this lesson the hard way several years ago when the company I worked for was acquired and my job was eliminated. Days later I attended a symposium for marketing leaders and when the first person I met asked me what I did, I froze like the proverbial deer in the headlights. I could no longer rely on the caché of working for a well-known global software company. Also, I could not very well say that I was a marketer—so was everyone else in the room. The truth was, I did not have an answer ready, and I stuttered and muttered until finally this kind woman looked me square in the eye and said, "You can't be it unless you can name it."

The lesson I learned that day has served me well ever since. You may discover that you need a few different pitches. For example, I have a version that emphasizes my professional speaking and another that emphasizes my company's consulting and training solutions. You will know that you have your pitch down pat when you can answer at least one of the following questions without batting an eye:

- What is your dream job?

- What do you do and why does it matter?

- What do you sell and who is your ideal client?

3. Get Digital

The "big three" social networks are LinkedIn®, Facebook® and Twitter®. When you are considering which one to join, think of them this way:

- **LinkedIn is a professional networking event.** Put on a suit, grab a stack of business cards and work the room with purpose.

- **Facebook is a backyard barbecue.** Throw on some shorts and a pair of flip-flops. The conversation is mostly social, although eventually someone asks you about work—hopefully there is a business card jammed in the back of your wallet. For more about how to use Facebook effectively, see *Social Capital* by Nannette Bosh on page 165.

- **Twitter is a cocktail party**. Wear something memorable, try to be scintillating and by all means, bring the conversation back to business. However, do not try to sell anything. No one likes being sold at a party. See *Twitter Strategies* by Gail Nott on page 175 for details on using Twitter effectively.

I ask my clients to focus first on LinkedIn because it is one of the most professional, robust and rapidly growing networks available.

LinkedIn boasts more than eighty million members and someone new joins the network every second of every day. Here is something else to know about LinkedIn: Google indexes every single profile page. That means that when I conduct an Internet search on your name, odds are I am going to find your LinkedIn profile if you have one. If you do not, I am going to wonder why not.

Optimizing your LinkedIn profile is one of the best ways to begin living your brand online. This is your chance to tell your professional story—take this opportunity to do just that.

4. Connect the Dots

Which would you prefer: 9 people keeping an ear to the ground for you or 90? What about 900? One of the aspects of social connectivity that tends to give networking novices cause to pause is the idea of scale. Simply put, the more people in your army of brand champions, the better. Many people are uncomfortable connecting with perfect strangers online. I agree that this approach can backfire if not managed properly. However, I would like you to consider connecting—or reconnecting as it were—with people you once knew, even if you are not currently in touch with them.

Remember that people buy from, hire and refer people they know, like and trust. If I knew you in high school, sang with you in the church choir, played intramural field hockey with you or babysat for your kids when I was in high school, then those are reasons to connect.

Have I lost you? Usually at this point in my keynote speech there is someone in the audience who mentally checks out because they cannot fathom connecting on LinkedIn, Facebook or the planet Mars with anyone from their distant past. However, I am living proof that with intentional social networking, even the thinnest thread can be reinforced and result in at least a referral.

Here is a case in point—my buddy Rob. He and I went to high school together a very, very long time ago. Two years ago we reconnected on Facebook, then LinkedIn—over the course of our online communication, Rob came to understand who I am now, what I do, and why I am special. As a result, when Rob's old friend called him and asked him if he knew anybody who advises companies and professionals on digital branding and communications, Rob said, "Sure, you should talk to my friend Sima." Just like that. Facebook— referral—money in my bank account. Are you with me?

5. Stay On Their Radar

When I meet someone at a networking event and have a meaningful conversation, I do not follow up via email—I reach out via LinkedIn. Once connected, I can make what I call "digital deposits" to keep my name high on his or her radar. A digital deposit is any action you take that puts your name in front of someone online. For example, you can post a birthday greeting on someone's Facebook wall. You might forward an invitation with a short note that says simply, "I saw this and thought of you."

Traditional networkers already embrace these behaviors. Savvy social networkers do it online for any number of reasons including speed, scale and reach. One of my favorite reasons is that the actions you take *inside* a social network bring people back to your profile, to your personal brand story. Don't forget, unless you choose a private channel, most actions you take within a social network are visible to everyone to whom you are connected. This may seem intrusive— however it actually serves to keep your profile high and your name top of mind.

6. Promote Brand You

Do you think self-promotion is difficult? Here is a new way to look at it:

- **Think *SEO*.** SEO stands for search engine optimization. Keywords matter, especially on LinkedIn. Start at the very top with your Headline, Summary and Specialties and then weave relevant keywords into your Experience and Interests. Many beginning networkers use their professional title in their LinkedIn Headline. For example, my title is President of Parlay Communications. However, that does not say much about my value proposition, does it? Instead, I use keywords to reinforce my value. Here is what you will find on my LinkedIn Profile: Marketing Consultant | Social Media Strategist | Networking Coach | Speaker | Trainer | LinkedIn Expert.

- **Think *share*.** Sharing information is a powerful way to attract targeted attention to your profile. Share news articles, special events or timely blog posts that you find interesting and that underscore your personal brand. All those widgets that enable sharing—use them. For example, I might use my LinkedIn status to share an article about social media that I think is well written. It doesn't need to be authored by me—it just needs to provide value and remind you what I do.

- **Think *status*.** Updating your status is one of the most underutilized ways to remind your network who you are, what you do, why you are special and even what you need. For example, if you are looking for work you might use your Facebook status to say that you are "prepping for an interview for an HR role at the University." I personally know at least a dozen people, myself included, who have found a job or client from a single status update.

- **Think *subtle*.** Remember that a little self-promotion goes a long way. Braggers are equally, if not more, annoying online than they are in person—perhaps because it is difficult to read humor or intention in short posts and status updates. The best way to shape your personal brand is to pay it forward. The old adage about "giving to get" is especially true within social networks where your actions are visible—and permanently recorded—for all to see. Ken Rochon covers this subject in his chapter, *An Unconditional Connector Is an Influential Connector* starting on page 47.

Take the Sway Factor™ Challenge

I often have to remind people that networking is an action verb. Intentional social networking works—if you work it. Countless people have told me that Facebook is just a waste of time, or that their LinkedIn profile has never generated even a single lead.

Networking in the digital age requires focus and energy. Crafting your story, completing your profile, connecting the dots and making purposeful updates will not come naturally to everyone. Yet with patience and practice, I believe everyone can be a networking ninja. Give it three weeks—what have you got to lose?

Start with LinkedIn and take the following six steps. Make a 21-day commitment, blocking out time on your calendar. Once you get the hang of it, social networking will become an extension of the way you work. Until then, make an appointment with yourself, be it fifteen minutes a day or just thirty minutes a week.

1. Complete your profile. Tell your story; brag a little. Remind your network who you are, what you do and why you are special.

2. Practice keyword density. Remember that your profile is indexed by Google. Use relevant keywords that pertain to your talent, industry or professional intent.

3. Update your status weekly. Updating your status is one of the simplest, quickest ways to keep your profile visibility high and underscore your personal brand position.

4. Aim for ten new contacts. Jump into the "way-back machine" and reconnect with old colleagues, past supervisors and long-lost friends. You will be surprised who you will find on LinkedIn.

5. Practice making digital deposits. At first this may seem awkward. Do not over-think it. Find a timely article and share the link. It can absolutely be that simple.

6. Be the brand. Allow your character, competency and charisma to shine through. Authenticity is critical to forging online relationships. Remember, the brand is you!

SIMA DAHL, MBA
Parlay Communications, Ltd.

Remember, the brand is you!

(312) 884-1888
sima@parlaycommunications.com
www.parlaycommunications.com

When Sima Dahl graduated from the University of Illinois in 1991 and started climbing the ladder at a Fortune 500 company, she soon learned a hard lesson not often taught in school—the importance of a strong personal brand and a professional network. Throughout her career in marketing and sales, she worked hard to develop these invaluable corporate skills. Today she is well-known for her Sway Factor™ system for social networking success and is one of the most sought-after thought leaders in the industry.

In 2008, Sima launched Parlay Communications to advise companies and professionals on digital branding and communications. Through her keynotes, corporate coaching and sales training, Sima has helped hundreds of job seekers, ladder climbers and rainmakers learn the art of online networking. Often referred to as the "Dale Carnegie of the Digital Age," Sima is known for her high-energy, no-nonsense approach to utilizing tools like LinkedIn and Facebook to forge a unique personal brand, create a strong professional network, and encourage business referrals.

Sima serves on several professional boards and is a bylined columnist for *Marketing News Magazine* and *Social Media Marketing Magazine*.

Social Capital
The New Business Building Tool
By Nannette Bosh, CPC

*I*n business, it is often said, "It's all about who you know." While your business is about more than that, networking—and building the right types of connections—is probably the single most powerful thing you can do for your business. Say goodbye to the days of hanging an "Open for Business" sign outside your door and say hello to the social media circuit networking scene.

Increasing your bottom line by building your own powerful and life changing connections through social media has become one of the most impactful tools you can use to build your business.

Getting the word out about you, your brand and your company by connecting with others through social media has become a business necessity. In real estate they say, "Location, location, location." If you are not already networking through the social media platforms, you need to be thinking "Facebook®, Twitter® and LinkedIn®." These are the best ways to make the lasting connections you need to help grow your business—taking it to new heights and increasing your net worth in the process.

Understanding the Opportunities on Facebook

Where can you go to conveniently network anywhere anytime and build connections that help build your business? Facebook is my personal favorite tool for building connections. In my opinion, Facebook, with its more than 500 million users and growing, is the number one social media networking platform and is worth every minute of time and effort you can spend there. Facebook offers the ability to network 24/7 from anywhere in the world with anyone in the world.

No need to dress to impress. From the comfort of your home, office or hotel room you can stay in constant direct contact with your entire network of connections while cultivating and making new ones. Facebook gives every user the chance to make friends with the movers and shakers from every industry. The potential to connect and meet some of the most important and influential people in the world is never more than one friend request away. This remarkable social media platform not only transformed my business—it changed my life.

Not long ago I thought of Facebook as "just a thing" high school and college kids were doing. When I signed up for an account of my own I realized that it is an amazingly powerful networking tool for building my business. Not only was I provided with the chance to connect with many wonderful and powerful people and make new friends daily, I was exposed to a world I never knew existed. An enormous amount of free information was at my fingertips, as well as access to guides, business assistance, tutorials, events, webinars, classes and online seminars—all offered to me by my new network of friends. In addition, of course, I had the opportunity to offer my business and services to them as well. If you have a Facebook account made up of a few college buddies and are using it to play games, then you may want to consider using it to its maximum potential—as a business-building tool.

If you are not on Facebook, I cannot stress enough the importance of taking this step. I highly recommend that you sign up today—it is free and easy to use. The people you meet and connect with on Facebook can become your new clients and support system and can provide you with sales or referrals and leads you can turn into sales. This is the only place where you can go to easily gain direct access to celebrities, television and radio personalities, producers, online magazine and newspaper editors, bloggers, authors and big players in every industry. I would wager to say that you cannot get that at your local chamber networking event.

Building Your Facebook Contacts

Ask not what your connections can do for you, but what you can do for your connections. Would you like to be surrounded by people who give the impression they are completely self-serving, or would you rather be surrounded by people who are giving and uplifting? Making friends on Facebook and immediately trying to sell them your products or services is not how you make and maintain friendships in real life. The same rule applies here. If you want to accumulate quality, beneficial relationship connections on Facebook that really count, you will not be building your friends list overnight. Have patience and do not be over eager. Although this kind of networking is a time-consuming process, it will be worth it in the end.

You cannot choose your family. However, you can choose your friends— now is your chance so choose them wisely. When sending a friend request, be sure to include a personal message along with your request. This increases the likelihood that the person will accept you into his or her Facebook family, especially if you have never actually met in person. When someone does accept you, it is common courtesy to send a personal message thanking that person for doing so. You can also post a thank you directly on their wall. Keep it friendly and acknowledging. This is not the time or place to post a blatant advertisement or plug for your business.

Now that you have been accepted, you can view the individual's personal information, wall posts and interactions with current friends. Take a genuine interest as you read and learn about your new friend. Visit his or her website and feel free to comment on some of his or her posts and photos. This shows you have a vested interest in what is going on in this person's life and business. Further, most people will return the favor. You get what you give. That being said, I encourage you to offer to help, assist, support and console members of your new network when appropriate, and in any way you can. If you see a chance to connect one of your Facebook friends with another so they might be able to build a mutually beneficial relationship, seize the moment, and they will both in turn do the same for you. Effective social media networking is all about giving first. You can cash in later on all that you have given.

Growing Your Facebook Network

Just having or opening a Facebook account is not enough to build and maintain excellent connections. Remember, this is your personal 24/7 networking event. You need to work your Facebook presence in a similar manner as you would work the room at your local chamber event. Do you stand quietly in the corner or do you bravely introduce yourself to others and work your way around the room? Hopefully, you introduce yourself to others and try to meet, connect and reconnect with as many people in the room as possible. This is the main point of networking. Facebook works the same way. You need to be willing to put yourself out there and make introductions when possible. If you have already established the connections you need, continue to cultivate and grow them.

Be your authentic self. No need to pretend to be someone you are not—we are all human with ups and downs, likes and dislikes. See *The Authentic Connection* by SherryLynn Wrenn and Sandra Fuentes on page 25 for more on this subject. It is in your best interest to share yourself, your life experiences, your joys—and sometimes sorrows—with your Facebook friends. They do not just want to see your business side. They want to know the real you. The rule of thumb is to make multiple personal posts for each single business or value-added post. When making non-personal posts, offer a mix of plugs for your business and new information of interest from your field of expertise. This is a great time to share a link to some recent information you have found to be a valuable resource to you or your business—hence the term "value-added" post. Your Facebook friends will be grateful. Always remember to conduct and portray yourself among your Facebook peers as you would at the office or at an in-person networking event. Upbeat posts and the display of an attitude of gratitude should make up most of your Facebook activity.

Keep in mind that you may be networking with people who are not in your time zone. Therefore, I recommend keeping your Facebook account open during the course of your work day— longer if possible. I also suggest checking it just as frequently if not more so than you do your emails. In fact, Facebook messaging has replaced almost all of my emailing. Be careful as you add friends and send requests to connect. If you attempt to send more than a few requests to connect per day, you will get a warning from Facebook. You may be withheld from sending more requests to connect for two or three days.

Making meaningful comments on others' posts is a great way to maintain constant contact, build real relationships and provide others the opportunity and desire to send you a request for friendship—simply because they liked your comment on the post you made on someone else's wall. That is a great way to grow your Facebook connections more rapidly. From personal experience I can tell you that daily networkers on Facebook love to see commenting or the use of the Like button on their wall just as you would enjoy seeing it on yours.

Your Networking Net Worth: Facebook, Twitter and LinkedIn

I recommend you also try Twitter and LinkedIn. This is the best way to determine which social platform will work best for you and your business. When you find your personal favorite you will most likely spend a lot of time there. Work it. If you feel comfortable with all of them, and you have the time to use all three, then I recommend you do so. Each offers different advantages. For example Twitter may not be as personal as Facebook. However, Twitter does not set limits on the number of connections you are allowed to make. Facebook does not allow you more than 5,000 connections. However, it does allow you to create a fan page for your business and you can have unlimited connections there.

Another great thing about Twitter is that your large number of followers will often share or "retweet" your posts and or blogs. You absolutely cannot beat free advertising. Do not forget to return the favor—social media favors carry huge weight among most all the members of these groups. See *Twitter Strategies* by Gail Nott on page 175 for an in-depth look at using Twitter.

Although I spend most of my time on Facebook simply because I love how truly personal it is, my social media network is not made up of Facebook alone. It also includes nearly 100,000 Twitter followers spread over several accounts, a Facebook Fan Page and a LinkedIn account.

You can grade, evaluate and assign an estimated dollar value based on the power of your connections through all of your accounts. However, *please* remember this important thing: while you are making the right connections, they are people and you cannot put a price tag on them or the value they may bring to you! Countless meaningful connections and life-changing opportunities have surfaced since I began to work the social media circuit. My personal Facebook account houses an enormous number of influential and well-known people.

Social Networking Can Change Your Life

I have had some life changing opportunities because I use these networking platforms to make incredible connections. Many of these opportunities stemmed from my "Elite" Facebook account, so let's start there.

1. The remarkable social media universe has somehow included me among the list of the Top 50 Facebook Elite, according to grader. com. If that is not a tremendous honor, I do not know what is. Feel free to grade your Facebook account on grader.com too.

2. I was given the unbelievable opportunity to speak on behalf of one of my high profile celebrity Facebook friends at a conference in front of nearly 600 women, and I was introduced by the celebrity herself. That day was surreal—it was at that very moment that I realized I wanted to speak publicly on a regular basis.

3. My business has been featured and promoted on television without paid advertising—negotiated by me through my own connections for free. I am not sure if you are familiar with the cost of running television ads. Segment exposure is far more valuable than running any advertisement. Sometimes there is a charge for segment exposure—it starts at approximately $5,000 and increases depending on the ratings of the program.

4. I have been interviewed on the radio at the request of my Facebook friends many times, sometimes for a full hour, and I never even had to make the request or ask for a favor. I was offered those privileges.

5. My business has been blogged about, talked about, tweeted and promoted by my Facebook friends and followers more times than I can possibly count, granting me business exposure and a multitude of Google® inbound links.

6. Due to the social media reach I now have, I was contacted by NBC in New York and invited to be a contributor on its latest project, *The Feast.* Of course I accepted!

7. My company's website traffic, sales and email list-building comes most often as a result of Facebook and Twitter directed visits. In fact, a large portion of our daily traffic returns to Facebook after they leave our site.

8. I became a Certified Professional Coach, as well as a trained public speaker, through my social media connections and the sharing of referrals.

9. I am a co-author of this book because—you guessed it—I was able to connect with the publisher through Facebook.

10. After I watched her for decades on *Good Morning America,* television host Joan Lunden provided the testimonial for my first book project. Joan and I originally met through Facebook and stayed connected. I was able to personally ask her myself if she would be willing to take a look at *My Style, My Way,* also published by THRIVE Publishing™, which of course includes a chapter written by me. She loved it and gave it her personal stamp of approval.

Through all of these incredible connections, my business and its products have been featured many times in newspapers and magazines—for *free!* I could go on and on. The main point is that you too can have all of this and more for yourself and your business. These are the same types of connections, opportunities and experiences that are available to you if you are willing to put the time in to use these types of social media networking platforms. From personal experience I can tell you that your life-changing connection is only a Facebook message or Tweet away. Believe it!

Nannette Bosh, CPC
Nannette Bosh Inc.

Building relationships and connections that change lives!

(860) 896-1208
nb@nannetteboshinc.com
www.nannetteboshinc.com

Featured countless times in print, radio and televised media, including a CBS *Primetime Special,* and reaching a social media audience of 125,000 and growing, Nannette knows how to network. Her direct connections to hundreds of celebrities, producers, television and radio personalities, online magazine and newspaper editors as well as bloggers and authors, has earned her a social media ranking among the Top 50 Facebook Elite.

While preparing to position her company, Bangle and Clutch, for a bright future on the web, Nannette discovered that she has more than a passion for fashion. She has a passion for connecting others, and as a result she has built a networking empire. She has turned her dedication to continuous networking into a business showcasing clients in front of her influential network, creating opportunities for them to gain tremendous media exposure, as well as establish the types of connections that change lives.

As a Certified Coach, author and speaker, it is Nannette's mission to assist others looking to build extraordinary relationships and connections for their life, their business and their success.

Twitter® Strategies
Secrets to Getting Connected and Getting Results
By Gail Nott

When I speak to entrepreneurs and business owners about what social media sites they use, they often portray Twitter as the ugly stepsister compared to other social networking sites. I hear phrases like, "It looks like a waste of time, It's just a bunch of teenagers," or the most popular statement, "I don't get it." Maybe it's the 140-character limit, the lack of closeness or the difficulty with following a conversation. I believe that the possibilities Twitter offers are simply misunderstood.

I have met countless valuable contacts on Twitter. I share information with them. I create strategic alliances with them. I help them promote their events and services to a wider audience that may not have been reached on Facebook®. Plus, I receive the occasional reply from a favorite celebrity—icing on the cake!

Think of Twitter as your radio station. If you send out great content—and we will get more into that later—you will get followers who want to hear more. In this way, Twitter is like a Facebook page. Instead of someone clicking on the *Like* button to subscribe to your page, they click on the *Follow* button. However, the most important difference about Twitter compared to other social media sites is that it is the only social media site, other than blogging, where every post is indexed by the search engines. This means that if someone searches for your business, they may find your one Facebook page. If you have a Twitter account and post multiple times about your business, it is possible to find *every, single post* in Google®. That is the real power of adding Twitter to your social networking efforts.

Connecting with People on Twitter

The first step in using Twitter is to complete your profile with your name, website link, bio and headshot. You can also upload a custom background image in which you also include your headshot, along with your logo and any relevant photos for your business. I suggest you use the same name and photo for all of your social media sites. This creates consistent branding and makes it easier for people to find and recognize you. Do not skip any of these basic steps. Your Twitter profile should clearly communicate who you are and what you do. For more about maximizing your profile, see *Networking in the Digital Age* by Sima Dahl on page 155.

I suggest turning off the email notifications to avoid getting hundreds of emails. Later, we will talk about how often to post on Twitter. If you do post consistently, which is the only way to get results from any marketing strategy, email notifications are not necessary.

Next, start following people you already know. If you use a Google or Yahoo® email address, you can have Twitter search through your address book and find people who are already on Twitter. If you do not use either service, it is easy to upload a comma-separated values (CSV) text file of your contacts into Google and then have Twitter search through your address book. The key contacts to focus on are your current clients, strategic alliances and prospects. In Twitter, you can add people to Lists, and you have the ability to make these lists public or private. Keep your lists of clients and prospects private, so that only you can see it. You can create a public list of your strategic alliances and give it a descriptive name that your audience would find interesting. For example, if you and your strategic alliances help "mompreneurs"—mothers who are also business owners—you can name your public list, "Mompreneur Resources."

Differentiate yourself. The Internet is cluttered with thousands of small businesses and entrepreneurs who say they do what you do. However, when you define a specific type of person and the specific problem you help that person solve, you can start to differentiate yourself from your competition. Imagine that you are talking to just one person. Who shows up in your mind when you think of your most ideal client? Ask yourself questions like: Is it a man or a woman? How old is he or she? Where does that person live? What are his or her interests? What is that person's main problem?

Target new contacts. Use either the Search feature on Twitter or Twitter's Advanced Search at search.twitter.com to find your ideal clients and start following them. Twitter's Advanced Search is a fantastic feature that allows you to target new contacts by what they post and where they are located. For example, if you are a massage therapist, you can search for the keywords *neck, back, pain,* and *hurts* within a radius of ten miles from your zip code.

Another way to find new contacts to follow on Twitter is to use their Who to Follow page. Twitter's software selects people for you to follow based on who you are following now, your location and their promoted or paid advertisers. You can also click on Browse Interests and you will see recommendations for top media personalities, news sites and industry experts.

Web directories like WeFollow® allow Twitter users to list themselves under chosen categories. You can list yourself, as well as find others to follow, based on similar industries, interests or your target market. Tweepi® is a web tool I recommend to help flush out spammers from your followers. You can also easily add new people to follow by groups versus adding them one by one.

You will find that a certain percentage of the people you follow will follow you back. Do not be dismayed if the numbers are not high as first. Aim for quality over quantity. Sending out high quality information in your posts can lead to higher quality followers.

It is very easy to get overwhelmed with all of the connections you will make on Twitter. Remember to continue using the Lists feature to stay in touch with your most important contacts. Add your new contacts to the appropriate lists too.

What to Post

The biggest key to success in using Twitter—and any social media site—is to give first and use the eighty/twenty rule. Spend eighty percent of the time sharing valuable content with your audience and networking with others. Spend the other twenty percent on promotion.

Post links to industry-related articles and blog posts that your audience would be interested in reading. If they have a Twitter name, be sure to mention their name with the @ symbol. For example, if your audience would be interested in reading about Internet marketing strategies, you can post a link to a blog post by a marketing coach and add "via @CoachTwitterName." You will be known as a resource in your field when you take the time to curate and aggregate niche content for your audience.

Make recommendations. By using #FollowFriday, or the #FF hashtag in your post, you can recommend people or businesses that you think other people should follow on Twitter. While you can mention several Twitter names in your post, I suggest that you pick only one person or business that you want to recommend at a time.

This might be one of your strategic alliances or one of your clients. Include his or her Twitter name with the @ symbol and say why you recommend that person. Posting an online testimonial on behalf of your network is in the true spirit of giving and can increase people's appreciation and respect for you.

Share ideas. Your giving activities can include your own work as well. Do you have a tip for the day or a new blog post? Just post what you are up to if you think your audience is interested in that. There is a common joke about Twitter that no one cares about what you had for lunch. However, I disagree with that if you are a nutritionist, a personal trainer, a restaurant owner or someone who supports local businesses. You can take your everyday events and relate them to what your audience is interested in hearing about. Are you working on a new presentation or a new product? Give your audience an inside peek into your day.

How Often Should You Tweet?

Post frequently. People frequently ask me how often should someone post on Twitter? Unlike other social networking sites like Facebook or LinkedIn, it is appropriate to post multiple times on Twitter every day. Some people even expect you to post multiple times. While there is no exact number of how many times you should post on Twitter, be careful not to go to the extreme—posting every minute of every day is too extreme. Your followers do not want you to flood the Timeline view of their Twitter home pages.

Tweet when you eat. If you only post once a day, it is unlikely that people will see your post. Your posting schedule also depends on your schedule. If you can only commit to five minutes a day on Twitter, then you can post your content, reply to followers and retweet other posts once a day for those five minutes. However, if you want massive results from using Twitter, I highly recommend spending at least five to ten minutes, several times a day. A common Twitter schedule is to tweet when you eat—log in to Twitter in the morning, at lunchtime and before or after dinner.

Your Twitter routine. When you log in to Twitter, quickly look at the first page of your home page, called the *Timeline*. Reply to or retweet any relevant tweets of the people you follow that your audience would also be interested in. Then reply to your Mentions, which are public tweets that include your Twitter username. This is like someone writing on your wall in Facebook. Direct Messages, or DMs, are private tweets people send directly to you. They are often automated messages and not really personal tweets to you. I recommend that you stay away from using automated tweets, and avoid responding to these since they are usually spam.

Remember to check on your lists of clients, strategic alliances and prospects. This will keep your most important contacts top of mind for you and their updates will not get lost in your home page. Click the Reply link to comment on a post they made or click the Retweet link to share something they posted. They will see that you are keeping in touch with them and will appreciate that you are sending their updates to your network. You can also welcome new followers, thank people for adding you to their lists, reply and retweet, and finally, post your content.

Once you are accustomed to this routine, it will not take you any longer than ten minutes each time. If you find yourself spending a lot more time than that, use a kitchen timer or a software program to keep your online time short and effective.

Twitter automation. Take advantage of technology to keep your Twitter posts consistent. Import your blog into Twitter with a tool like Twitterfeed®. Every new blog post will automatically post on Twitter. I suggest setting it up so that it posts your blog title, part of the first sentence and, of course, a link to your blog so your Twitter followers can read the rest on your website. Some social media tools, like HootSuite®, allow you to upload a spreadsheet of updates that you can schedule out for the future. This is very convenient. However, do not use this as a crutch. You can attract more Twitter followers if you take the time to engage with people online personally. Nobody wants to do business with a robot.

Likewise, be mindful of software that automatically sends a direct message to new followers. Even though you can personalize the message with their name, it can still feel robotic if it is too pushy or too common. "Thanks for following me. Get my free ebook . . . " is so common that it is not only ineffective, it also may rub your new followers the wrong way, and they may become your new *unfollowers* instead.

Outsource. If you are busy already and not sure how you can fit Twitter into your day, you can outsource and delegate part of the work. Social media management is a specialty in the marketing field, as well as in the virtual assistant world. You can outsource the technical aspects, including integrating Twitter into your other social media sites, as well as administrative tasks like data entry and deleting spam.

Getting Results

Going back to the eighty/twenty rule, remember to use twenty percent of your posts to promote your own services, products and events. Rather than asking people for a direct purchase on Twitter, share a catchy title and a link to your sales or registration page. For example, "Overwhelmed with your to-do-list? Http://yourlink.com" would be a catchy tweet to promote a time management coach's services. If you are looking for speaking engagements, ask for connections, send tweets about your speaking topics, promote your upcoming presentations and post links to your speaking page on your website. See *Use Speaking to Build a Thriving Network* by Caterina Rando on page 209 for more about growing your speaking career.

Speaking of your website, make sure the landing page you send people to has a clear call to action. If you are promoting your upcoming workshop and the page you send people to is your home page and not the registration or sales page, people can get lost or distracted and may never sign up for your workshop. An effective landing page should build an emotional connection with the audience and give them a reason to purchase or sign up. For more on events, see *Using Virtual Events to Build Your Network* by Lynn Pearce on page 185.

Give something away. Another way to increase your results with Twitter is to build your mailing list by giving away something for free. Create a free report that people can get when they sign up, and promote the report on Twitter with a compelling post to get people's attention. What problem does your ideal client have? Reference that problem in your tweet and provide solutions in your free report— without giving everything away. Tell them *what* the solutions are, not *how* to solve the problem. If they are interested in *how* to solve the problem, offer them a consultation.

As you can see, Twitter can be a waste of time or a gold mine. It all depends on how you use it. If you choose to utilize Twitter by becoming known as a valuable resource and by consistently engaging with your network, you can expect your efforts to pay off.

Remember these steps for successful Twitter results:

• Fill out your profile completely to brand you and your business.

• Start connecting with people you already know, including your current clients, strategic alliances and your prospects.

- Find new contacts using Search, Suggestions and other Twitter-related websites.

- Remember the eighty/twenty rule when posting. Have a giving and educational mindset.

- Post consistently, taking advantage of technology to help you. However, remember that personal engagement is necessary for success.

- When directing people to your website, have a clear call to action, whether it is giving them a free gift to add them to your email list or registering them for your workshop.

Implement these strategies to make your connections count on Twitter!

GAIL NOTT
Nott Ltd Solutions

*You download your passion,
we upload your message!*

(925) 709-4245
gail@gailnott.com
www.gailnott.com

Gail Nott is a specialist in social media and relationship marketing. Her company, Nott Ltd Solutions, manages Internet marketing campaigns for businesses large and small throughout California. Gail has experience in web development, search engine optimization and social media strategies. She was a recipient of the Constant Contact® All-Star Award for two years in a row for demonstrating best practices in the effective use of email marketing.

Gail helps her clients turn their business goals into actionable plans and marketing strategies that pay off. Her clients learn how to focus their social networking efforts to develop both "word of mouth" and "speed of light" marketing, using the right sites and systems to their professional advantage. Gail uses her passion for social media to help others by dispelling the mystery and filtering out the hype of this marketing tool. She shows business owners how authenticity, a giving mindset and relationship-building are the keys to successful social media marketing.

Gail lives in Concord, California, with her husband Cory and her stepson Cody. She enjoys reading, singing, hiking, and camping—when she's not online.

Using Virtual Events to Build Your Network

Five Simple Steps for Success

By Lynn Pearce

Your greatest business asset is your list—your network of customers, prospects and anyone who wants to hear from you about your business. I advise you to nurture and feed your list so that people will want to stay in contact with you. One of the best ways to grow your business is to grow your list, and one of the quickest ways to build your list is by holding a virtual event. In less than a month, you can double or even triple the size of your list.

Most people think of virtual events as teleseminars or webinars. While that is true, it is also limited in scope. Teleseminars and webinars are just channels for you to reach your audience during an event. It is similar to describing vacations as cruises or resorts. As we know, there are many more possible types of vacations you can take.

Consider the meaning of the two words *virtual* and *event*. *Virtual* means that we don't have to be in a specific physical location to take part or attend. *Event* refers to a planned public or social occasion. Open your mind to other possible virtual events. How about a virtual book launch or tour, a virtual networking event, a virtual treasure hunt, a virtual birthday party, a virtual concert, a virtual spa day or even a virtual retreat?

Here are five simple steps you can take to produce successful virtual events. With a little forethought and planning, you can build your list in a big way and expand your network with people who want to be part of what you are doing and who want to hear more from you.

Step 1: Motivation—Why Hold a Virtual Event?

The first step is to determine your reasons or motivation for holding a virtual event. Besides wanting to grow your list, consider what else is important to you. For most people, these reasons fall into one or more of three categories:

• To make money

• To increase your credibility or standing as an expert

• To create information products

Once you determine your reasons, you can use them to define the success criteria for your event. If you want to make money, ask yourself how much money you want to make and within what timeframe. If you want to create products, ask yourself what they look like and if there is a market for them. If you want to increase your credibility or your visibility, ask yourself how you want to be perceived after the event and who will you know who you didn't know before.

By defining these criteria, you will know what goals you are aiming for and you will easily be able to measure your success after the event. You will also know when you are done with the project—your goals are met—and you will have enough information to determine if you want to do it again.

Growing your list. Since this is your main reason for having a virtual event, let's get into a little more detail about this area. Consider these questions:

- How much do you want to grow your list—50 percent or 500 percent?

- How many people would that be—100 or 1000?

- Does everyone new to your list need to be a customer? For example, must they have paid you in exchange for something of value or can they simply show interest in what you have to offer and want to stay in touch?

- How can you reach a bigger audience of potential prospects?

- What will you do for the new people on your list after the event?

- Can the speakers at your event help grow your list?

- Who else could help?

- If you are only interested in growing your list, should your event be free—and if so, how will you cover your costs?

By identifying *what* you want out of the event, you can trick your brain into doing what it is extraordinarily good at—looking for solutions to a problem. You do not need immediate answers. However, you can "seed" your brain so that unconsciously it starts to seek answers for you.

Step 2: Market Research—What Will Make People Show Up?

There are two sides to market research when planning a virtual event. The internal side looks at the subject matter for your event. The external side looks at what other people are doing around that particular subject area.

Internal market research. Creating a virtual event that no one attended would be sad—like hosting a party with no guests! When you planned your party, you did not realize that there was another event that night to which most of your friends would go. You decided on sushi without remembering that most of the folks you invited are vegetarian. You booked a DJ who specializes in '70s disco music, forgetting that your friends are all under 40 and have never even heard of *Saturday Night Fever*.

Surprisingly, many people do this when designing virtual events. Instead of designing for their audience, they design for themselves and then wonder why they did not get more signups or rave reviews for their amazing offer. Unfortunately, their offer was only amazing for *them*. Being the audience at your own event does not count.

How do you get it right? Just ask! Reach out to your existing list. Ask your Facebook® friends and fans. Ask on Twitter®. Ask a related group on LinkedIn®. Ask them, "If I could tell you one thing about [your specialty or niche—the subject of your virtual event], what would that be?"

If you do not have a list or don't belong to a social network, think about who your ideal attendees would be and find out where they hang out online. In what groups or forums do they participate? Find out what problems they are asking for help with.

Use what you learn to drive the subject of your event. Use your research to learn what keeps people in your target market awake at night. Design an event that meets your audience's needs. You may even get suggestions about who your audience wants to hear from. Those would be your ideal speakers.

Simply considering what people want, rather than what you think is a good idea, can be one of the strongest drivers in getting people to sign up for your event and join your list.

External market research. Once you know what your audience wants, find out what the competition is up to—without getting discouraged and giving up thinking that someone else is already doing what you want to do. If that were the case, we would all be driving black Model T Fords®!

This is where great innovations occur. Look at what is already out there. Then figure out a new and different way to meet the needs of your audience. Be innovative! Define the key differentiators which will become the core elements of your marketing message.

Let's say you work with stay-at-home moms (SAHMs), helping them find home-based businesses that meet their specific needs. You already know the problems they face, including making sales and how to run a business. Through your external market research you can see that plenty of people offer virtual events about marketing and getting clients. There it is staring you in the face—an event all about business basics: *Accounting 101, Inc Versus LLC, How to Find Good Virtual Assistance.*

That's just one example. Observe what your competition or others in your industry already offer and you will discover what you have or can do that is different and could be a big hit.

Once you have completed your internal and external market research, you can easily compile it into a succinct event outline.

• Your target market

• The problems you can help them solve

• Your event title

• What makes your event different and has it stand out from the crowd

• Event topics and speakers to invite

This information is vital when it comes to putting together the materials you will need once you define your marketing strategies.

Step 3: Marketing—Create Your Virtual Event Marketing Plan

There is nothing really scary about marketing. It is just deciding how you will let people know about your event. What channels can you use to reach potential attendees, how many people can you reach through each channel, how much will it cost to make contact through each channel and what will that contact look like?

Consider these channels:

• Twitter

• Facebook

• LinkedIn

• Other online communities where you are active—for example Ning® groups and Foursquare®

• Your email list

• Online advertising

• Direct mail

• Groups and associations to which you belong—professional or otherwise

Let's say your business has 500 Facebook fans. The cost to reach out to them is the time it takes you or a virtual assistant (VA) to craft an invitation and post it to your fan page to promote the event. If you post it three times with minor tweaks to the content, the cost might be $50 for an hour of VA time.

Repeat this process for each of your channels to find where you can get the most reach for the least amount of money. This helps you prioritize where to spend your marketing time and dollars.

Once you lay out your marketing plan, answer the question from Step 1, "Is my reach big enough to help me meet my goals?"

If the answer is no, then consider finding some joint venture (JV) partners.

- **Ask your speakers to promote your event.** However, do not assume that they will actually follow through—even if you offer them a split on earnings.

- **Ask people in your network** who have an audience who would be interested in your event.

- **Find and ask people you don't know** who have big lists and might be interested in promoting you because their list would be interested in the event and the added value you have to offer.

For each potential JV partner, go through the same exercise you did for yourself. This helps you prioritize potential partners and test to see if having that partner would help you meet your goals. You also end up with a pretty comprehensive plan of what marketing materials you will need to create to promote your event effectively.

Step 4: Money—How Much Is This Going to Cost and What Is the Potential Income?

In this step, look at both sides of the equation. How much will it cost to put on the virtual event and how much money can you realistically earn from the event to meet those costs and earn enough profit to meet your goals?

First, determine your offer. What will people who sign up for your event receive in exchange for, at a minimum, their email addresses and their precious time and perhaps their hard-earned cash?

Marketing professionals say that a confused mind will not buy. Therefore, you want to define three offers—each containing progressively more value than the last. That gives people choices without confusing them.

For example, one offer may include being able to listen to your speakers for up to 24 hours after the initial broadcast. The next offer may provide a longer access period—perhaps up to a month. The highest value offer may include downloads of the recordings.

Second, decide what to charge people for each offer. Your market research will help here. Your audience may tell you how much they value having their problems solved—what your competition has already done may tell you what the market will bear.

Next, make two lists: what will make you money and what will cost you money?

On the Making Money list expect to see income from:

• People buying your offers. Use your "reach" numbers for each channel and your offer price to calculate the projected amount.

• Funds you specifically set aside for the event. It is unusual to treat this as income. However, you are creating an event budget here, not a budget for your whole business. This approach will give you a more accurate picture for the event.

• Sponsors or other investors

• Product sales created as a result of the event

On the Spending Money list expect to see the cost of:

- Any technology you need to host the event—like bridge lines, conference services and website development

- Any assistance you need to make the event happen—like graphic designers, virtual assistants and technology experts

- Packages you provide to the people who signed up for your event— like the cost of creating CDs, transcripts, mp3s, binders, and shipping and handling

- Affiliate fees you owe those who helped promote your event

Subtract the Spending Money total from the Making Money total to see whether you will make a profit or have a loss. The total is an estimate designed to help you decide if it is worth more of your time—and maybe money—to make the event happen.

As a result of this calculation, if you are seeing a loss, you may want to re-think some aspects of your event and how it is marketed. It is better to be forewarned of a potential disaster than to discover a loss when it is too late to make any changes.

Step 5: Making it Happen—Designing Your Virtual Event

Finally we get to what most people jump to first—planning the virtual event. Think how much better informed you are and ready to proceed having done all of the above research and thinking up front. This makes the planning stage comparatively simple.

First, think of all the responsibilities related to the event. This is the high-level task list for your project. I suggest you categorize the responsibilities using the following questions:

- How do you acquire the content to present at your event? For example, how are you going to invite speakers, get their materials and/or create special materials?

- How do you let people know about the event and how do they sign up? For example, how are you going to contact JV partners, create marketing copy and set up your shopping cart?

- How will you enable people who have signed up to attend the event and listen to or watch the speakers in action?

- How will you keep attendees fully engaged and happy during the event?

- How will you show those who expressed interest in the event that you care for them after the event is over? Remember, you have their email addresses.

Next, look at how your answers to the above questions fit into each of these phases:

- Launch

- Promotion and marketing

- The event itself

- Post-event

Now that you are aware of the details necessary to make the event happen, take a deep breath. Determine what help you need. Does your Spending Money list need revising to include the help? Does this make you reconsider the event in any way? Do you need more JV partners? Would you get more attendees if you changed the offer pricing? Ultimately, will you meet your goals? Looking at the entire picture, make an informed decision as to whether this is the right strategy for your business at this time. If all signs point to yes, then the final step is to plan out each phase on your calendar and get started!

After the Planning—What's Next?

You've done all the heavy lifting by designing your virtual event. Now it is time for the easy part—good old-fashioned execution! If you work on your own, the virtual event plan provides a very clear picture of exactly what you need to do. If you work with an online business manager or virtual assistant, the plan shows them exactly what you need them to do. The plan becomes the single point of reference that enables your whole team to be able to work together efficiently and effectively, avoiding any misunderstandings.

Use the above five steps to plan a virtual event that can quickly double or even triple the size of your list, be an additional income source and increase your credibility and visibility in your industry. Good luck with your event—I'm looking forward to seeing an invitation in my inbox very soon!

LYNN PEARCE
Managing Partner
The Calisto Group LLC

*Your best kept secret
for virtual event success*

(415) 287-0807
lynn.pearce@thecalistogroup.com
www.virtualeventmaven.com

When Lynn Pearce, founder of The Calisto Group, graduated from college and started work as a software engineer, she discovered that she was a very effective bridge between technology and business—two worlds that usually do not speak the same language. Working as a management consultant, she has helped organizations design better computer systems, build more useful products and define more efficient business processes in fields as diverse as agriculture, banking/finance, broadcasting, construction, education, health care, insurance, retail, semiconductors, telecommunications and utilities.

In 2008, Lynn launched The Calisto Group with the goal of bringing corporate best practices to small businesses and entrepreneurs. "There are plenty of people out there telling you how to market your business, but very few who can really help you establish a foundation upon which you can build for real growth."

Lynn actively works with a few select clients as an online business manager (OBM) and specializes in helping entrepreneurs use virtual events as a key element in their business strategy to deliver outstanding value to their customer base and achieve their business goals quickly and easily.

Build Connections Quickly with Your Own Talk Radio Show

By Ana Lucia Novak

*T*echnology in the 21st century has made it possible for small business owners to reach and connect with more people by leveraging major social media platforms such as Twitter®, Facebook®, LinkedIn® and YouTube®. People buy from those they know, like and trust, and these platforms enable people to get to know you before they buy from you.

Therefore, it is important to educate, add value and help people have instant access to you in order to foster relationships so that prospects convert to clients. Social media has paved the way to connect, engage and demonstrate your expertise to your target audience in real time, while staying in touch with your current clients. However, there is another avenue that can build connections and impact your online presence—hosting your own online talk radio show.

"Blogging doesn't have to be in text. Here is a social radio network where bloggers use voice to quickly connect with their audience."
—Renee Hopkins Callahan, American blog author and editor

Using online radio to connect with people has a unique benefit that other online avenues do not. People can more easily resonate with your message when they hear your stories through your spoken words and your tone. Having an online talk radio program is an opportunity to reach a different, highly targeted audience that does not necessarily use social media platforms, or at minimum prefers radio. With online radio, you can take advantage of instant access to the Internet via mp3 players, pad devices, tablets and smart phones.

Online Radio—A Trend Worth Following

With radio, we have an opportunity to create deep and lasting connections and reach quality people in a short amount of time. According to a 2010 study from Bridge Ratings LLC, the number of online radio listeners is growing by leaps and bounds. By 2020, 185 million people will be listening to Internet radio. That means the number of people listening today will more than double in ten years! Other studies show the phenomenal growth of online radio participation, such as *The Infinite Dial 2009* study by Arbitron/Edison, which indicates distinct increases in online radio listeners. For example:

• Weekly online radio audience numbers exploded in the last year, to about 42 million Americans aged twelve and older. One in five Americans aged 25 to 54 years old listen to online radio on a weekly basis.

• In one month, 69 million Americans listened to talk radio.

• In one year, the size of the weekly online radio audience rose by nearly one-third.

• Online radio clearly attracks an upscale, well-educated, high-income audience.

• Variety and control are top reasons for listening to online radio.

• Online radio is the soundtrack for research and shopping on the Internet.

• Radio's digital platforms provide advertisers with new touch points to reach desirable targets.

- Americans are exercising more control over their use of media—think smart phones and mp3 players.

- Consumers expect to find their content online.

These statistics offer the promise that hosting your talk radio show can open up avenues to your target market, paving the way to meet, connect, engage and foster new relationships.

Are you wondering how on earth you are going to sustain a weekly radio show? Your guests are right under your nose! Start with your own sphere of influence on Twitter, Facebook, LinkedIn, Meetups®, BNI®, NAWBO® along with your local community business leaders. Each one has a story worth sharing over talk radio that will resonate and connect with your audience. In one segment, I featured Patty Farmer, The Networking CEO, and we discussed various methods for an introvert to successfully connect with people at a busy networking event. She offered insight and tips, such as bringing a friend or wearing a bold print, scarf or jewelry that could be a conversation starter. Patty later shared that a listener emailed her to thank her for the inspiration and motivation to start getting out there networking with new people. For more insights from Patty, see her chapter on page 109 in this book: *Getting the Most out of Your Networking Organizations.*

The Benefits of Hosting Your Own Talk Radio Show

Besides providing rich, rewarding and exciting opportunities to grow and expand your network, you can carve out opportunities to become acquainted with other thought leaders, opening the door to potential strategic alliances and joint ventures. People remember thoughtful and considerate acts of kindness. Hosting a talk radio show is another way to give back to your community by endorsing people within your sphere of influence. Use your talk radio show to feature solopreneurs with unique business service offerings. This can then provide more business opportunities for you as you get access to their world.

In addition, hosting your own show:

- Gives you the power and flexibility to promote your products, services, website and perhaps your newly published book

- Carves a niche for you in your industry, establishing your credibility and authority

- Gets you free exposure and publicity when you use social media to promote your show

- Offers valuable information that will elevate your reputation, with increased respect and prestige among your peers

- Provides new expanded opportunities, both personally and professionally

How to Start Your Online Radio Show

There are several online talk radio show systems you can use to get started. I prefer BlogTalkRadio^{SM} because it is easy to use, has free and affordable plans and gives you control over your webpage and schedule. According to its website at www.blogtalkradio.com, it is, ". . . the social Internet radio network that allows users to connect quickly and directly with their audience. Using an ordinary telephone and computer, hosts can create free, live, call-in talk shows with unlimited participants that are automatically archived and made available as podcasts. No software download is required. Listeners can subscribe to shows via RSS in iTunes® and other feed readers."

BlogTalkRadio is social media enabled—you can easily connect and share your show on Twitter and Facebook. You can set reminders in BlogTalkRadio that push out reminders to your Twitter account and Facebook profile an hour before your talk radio show. You can promote the link on multiple social sites using the Share button, making it feasible to announce the topic, day and time within multiple LinkedIn groups with a click of a button. You can also link it to the Digg®, Stumbleupon® and Delicious® websites. The same link is good before, during and after the show, and it can be used to complement your blog post. You can add a widget to your Facebook via the Wildfire® app. You can also add your RSS feed to iTunes and a number of podcast directories, creating awareness and directing traffic back to your talk radio show.

Many people do not consider hosting their own radio show as a complement to their marketing efforts. They may think it would be too hard to get into the online radio industry. In fact, it is so easy and simple that you can start your own show tonight!

I first learned about BlogTalkRadio when I was asked to be a guest on the *Social Media Paradigm Blog Talk Radio Show* hosted by Dino White, who inspired me to start my own talk radio show. I decided to complement my Meetup group with a show featuring local, savvy business leaders. This pushed me out of my comfort zone—I had to reach out and invite people I had never met to be guests on my show.

Setting up an account with BlogTalkRadio is easy. It offers a free plan and premium plans. I suggest you start with the free plan— it allows five callers and an unlimited amount of online listeners. Premium (paid) features offer:

• Enhanced switchboard

• Upload, edit and replace episodes

• Host with Skype®

• Prime time scheduling

• Priority support

- Enhanced reporting

- Host a 2- or 3-hour show per day

- From 50 to 250 live, concurrent callers

- From 5,000 to 20,000 impressions per month

Be seen as the expert who cares enough to educate, inform and add value to your clients and prospects. Approach doing an online talk radio show with the mindset that you are helping people access, know, like and trust you as the go-to resource person. The more they hear from you through social media channels and radio, the more they will connect with you and begin to rely on you. Social media marketing adds to your online marketing efforts. Radio is an effective marketing tactic used to reach a wider audience and to earn recognition, expert status and awareness of your services and products.

You can make real connections using radio because listeners get to know the real you, allowing you to transform relationships from acquaintances to deep personal connections. I have found that online radio creates the opportunity to meet quality leaders and experts from all walks of life. Plus, having your own online radio show:

- Gives you the ability to influence many—and not just the day of the show

- Allows you to place recordings on your site and share them across social media platforms, thus building your brand and gaining exposure to new people

- Offers the freedom to create a unique, branded, personalized profile

- Provides the flexibility to be on the air any time of the day or week

- Lets you decide when, where and how to share your information

- Gives people instant access to you and your guest as you share your knowledge, tips and expertise

Take Action Now!

Start hosting a weekly or bi-monthly talk radio show today. Here's how to get started:

Create a list of potential guests. Scope out your LinkedIn network, leverage LinkedIn groups, consider your Facebook page fans and look at Twitter lists. Don't forget Meetup, eWomenNetwork®, Ladies Who Launch® and Hatch Network®.

Select a day of the week and a time that works for you—be consistent.

Compose an email to your inner circle. Let people in your world know you are hosting a show. List the date, time and theme of your show. Ask people to apply to be guest speakers and to recommend people in their world.

Book your guests in advance. Create an editorial calendar and update it frequently. Promote it on your Facebook event tab, LinkedIn Events tab, Plancast.com®, EventBrite.com® and EventSync® which will automatically submit to Upcoming® and Eventful®.

Add the RSS feed to iTunes and podcast listings. Cast a wide net and submit your RSS feed to these directories:

- www.podcast.com

- www.podcastlikethat.com/ping

- www.blubrry.com

- www.odeo.com

- www.podcastalley.com

- www.podcastpickle.com

- www.podcastdirectory.com

- www.syndic8.com

Add a widget to your website and Facebook page. BlogTalkRadio provides you with the basic HTML code to add a widget to your website. You can also connect it to Facebook, which updates your wall before and after your show.

Write and submit a weekly press release announcing your talk radio show, the topic and your guest. You can submit it to free press release sites. You can also write a short summary of the show as a blog post and link it to the radio show. This is great for link backs as well as giving your audience instant updates. Your guests will remember you for your time and generosity promoting them via these tactics.

Find a co-host who can rotate with you and help cover any costs. A co-host can help fill up your editorial calendar and offer variety to your show. He or she can also split the cost of a premium plan—a win-win arrangement.

Create an editorial calendar and share it everywhere. An editorial calendar not only makes it easy to plan and prepare the necessary steps to gain exposure for your show. It will let your audience know what you have planned, generating future interest in upcoming guests and topics. Share your editorial information through the following methods:

- Post each show as a Facebook Page event.

- Update your Facebook fans using the Submit Note section.

- Post each show as a LinkedIn event.

- Share the topic, date, time and name of your guest within applicable LinkedIn groups.

- Send an email update to your LinkedIn network.

- Submit the event to Plancast at www.plancast.com, which is synced with Twitter and Facebook. This notifies your followers and fans who are also subscribed to plancast.com.

- Submit the event to Eventbrite® at www.eventbrite.com—an online public, free directory. Include appropriate categories, tag words and keywords.

- Submit the event to EventSync at www.eventsync.com, which also updates online submission sites, including Upcoming and Eventful.

- Set up automated tweets to post one week in advance, a few days in advance and the day of your show.

- Submit a fresh press release to free press release sites each week announcing your guest, topic and information. Make each press release newsworthy with an angle that will get the media's attention.

Ideally, line up your guests in advance, so you can complete all of these activities upfront. Also, think about hiring a virtual assistant to partner with you to make this process easier to manage. Consistency with these steps will help people find you and your show, drive traffic to your website and grow your reputation as a thought leader who helps others succeed.

Nothing to Lose and Much to Gain

You want to make your connections count and you can use radio to affect someone's life or business with your story—and the stories of your guests. Proper planning, strategy, tactics and execution will guarantee a sense of accomplishment as your talk radio show begins to gain popularity. There is no one in the world like you, and there is someone in the world waiting to meet you. Imagine the surprises that could await you each week as you begin this journey into co-creating a rich airwave filled with laughter, inspiration and motivation. You have nothing to lose and everything to gain by starting your own talk radio show. Do not let fear of the unknown stop you from this exciting journey into success.

ANA LUCIA NOVAK
Social Media Tech Solutions

Wrap your arms around social media

(650) 771-0777
ana@socialana.com
www.socialana.com

Ana Lucia Novak has over twenty years of high tech industry experience in Silicon Valley and with hot start-up companies. She is a Silicon Valley social media marketing specialist and a catalyst for change.

Ana Lucia thrives on solving problems for her clients, streamlining business processes and systems and freeing her clients from behind-the-scenes operations so they can focus on creating products, building their brand and increasing revenue. She has knowledge and hands-on experience with social media infrastructure set-up, as well as creating and executing social media strategy, Internet marketing, search engine optimization (SEO) and WordPress® sites. She is known as a dynamo, a motivator and a woman of action. Her invaluable experience in marketing, business development, human resources and operations offers unique value to anyone who seeks her as a venture partner. She wastes no time getting her clients up to speed, kick-starting their online presence, promoting them through various online channels and providing inspiration and creativity for informational products.

Ana Lucia hosts two weekly BlogTalkRadio™ shows: *Savvy Business Leaders* and *Social Media Happy Hour*. She enjoys spending time with her husband, practicing Bikrum yoga and reading.

Use Speaking to Build a Thriving Network

By Caterina Rando, MA, MCC

At any event, it is better to be in the front of the room speaking than in the back of the room listening! Why? When you are the speaker, you open the door wide to making many new, wonderful contacts who can quickly lead to new clients and a more thriving business.

Speaking is one of the fastest, easiest and most productive ways of generating leads and having customers and clients come to you. When you are the speaker, you are the one who comes home with the most business and the most new contacts. When you are the speaker everyone in the room meets you, even if you do not have a chance to individually meet everyone. You get the most exposure, and you are positioned as the expert in the room.

If you already are a speaker, I am going to give you some tips for improving your ability to build your network when you speak. If you do not already speak, I will share with you what to do to begin building a thriving network through speaking.

Using Speaking to Build Strategic Alliances

No matter how competent you are, you cannot grow your business if you stay in touch with only clients, past clients and people who have expressed an interest in working with you. Make sure your marketing activities include a way to gather new contact information from people who are interested in what you do, not just those who already have benefited from what you have to offer. I encourage all my clients to build strategic alliances with other service providers for everyone's mutual benefit.

What do I mean by a strategic alliance? I am talking about creating a relationship with an individual or company that has the same ideal client as you, yet provides a different product or service. Your businesses complement each other because your clients will most likely also need what your strategic alliances have to offer and *vice versa*. These are the types of partners with whom you want to meet and partner. For example, in my publishing business, THRIVE Publishing™, we create books that build businesses, and most of our clients are entrepreneurs. Therefore, great strategic alliance partners for me are companies and individuals that also work with entrepreneurs, such as website development companies, sales training companies, small business attorneys and accountants. We all have the same client groups, yet we do something different for them.

Ask yourself a few key questions to determine who are the best strategic alliance partners for you:

- What other services and products do my clients need?

- Who do I know that provides these products or services?

- Who else can I get to know that provides these products or services?

When you answer these questions, you will begin to identify the types of strategic alliances you want to make. After you define your ideal strategic alliance partners and identify the individuals in those categories, contact them and let them know that you would like to explore forging strategic alliances with them.

How does all of this relate to using speaking to grow your network? Once you have your strategic alliance partners, you can host each other at a workshop for the other's clients. You can also do a workshop together where you both promote to your lists. When you do this, you know you will be in front of people who need what you have to offer. What could be better?

Start now. Invite a strategic alliance partner to collaborate with you. Use speaking or presenting a workshop to get in front of each other's clients—and watch your business soar.

Create a Speaker Sheet to Get Booked with Ease

"Speech is power: speech is to persuade, to convert, to compel."
—Ralph Waldo Emerson,
American lecturer, philosopher, essayist and poet

As I mentioned, speaking is an excellent way to showcase your expertise and meet people. In order to get speaking engagements, you need a speaker sheet. This is a one-page description of you, your topic and the benefits the audience will get from this topic. You use your speaker sheet to differentiate yourself from every other consultant or service provider who wants to speak and does not have any marketing information specifically designed to get her booked as a speaker. Your speaker sheet makes a big difference. For more about standing out in your market, see *Professional Presence and Visual Impact* by Lori Barber on page 13.

Decide what you are going to talk about and choose a topic that interests the groups where your potential clients gather. Your talk also has to showcase you and your expertise. For example, if you are an image consultant and your ideal clients are career women, you could present on the topic of "How to Look Great and Be Confident in Any Business Situation."

Once you are clear on your ideal client and your presentation topic, write up your complete speaker sheet.

Here are the elements of a speaker sheet:

- Catchy title at the top. Most people probably do not recognize your name, and it will not capture attention. Start your speaker sheet with a catchy phrase or a phrase that clearly captures the benefits of your speech. Emphasize what audience members will get. For example, a client of mine gives a speech with the catchy title "Becoming Great with Money."

- Your name follows the title.

- A description of yourself as a speaker and your credentials

- A list of topics you speak on and the benefits of each topic

- Testimonials and a client list if you have them

- Your contact information

In addition to your speaker sheet, also add a speaker page on your website to position you as a speaker. This is key if you want people to call you to speak.

Reach out to the Right Groups

Once you are clear on your ideal client and have created your speaker sheet, ask yourself where your potential clients gather. Then put together a list of organizations in your area where your potential clients meet. Contact these groups by phone or send an email with your speaker sheet attached as a PDF with a link to your website. Let them know you have a presentation that would be of great interest to their members.

Customize your email to match your speech and the audience. Make sure you include your complete contact information and enable all hyperlinks. After a few days, if you have not received a response, follow up with a phone call.

Getting booked as a speaker takes lots of follow-up, and you may want to delegate this task to someone on your team. Once an organization is interested in booking you, get on the phone personally and let them know more about what you are going to do.

Your speech must be full of valuable information. Even if audience members do not hire you, they will feel great about what they have learned from you. Take a couple of minutes at the end of your talk to make a clear and specific offer that audience members can take advantage of that day.

Set Yourself Up for Success

Speaking is more than just showing up and talking to the audience. A successful speech requires research and preparation. Find out everything you can about a group to make sure it is the right match for you. You will probably speak to someone at the organization who is in charge of bringing in speakers. Make sure you get the answers to the following questions:

• **Who will be in the audience?** Look to meet potential strategic alliance partners and potential clients.

• **How far will you have to travel to deliver the speech?** You need to take time away from your business to prepare your speech and then travel and present your speech.

- **How much time do you have to talk?** Always ask for more time. The more time people spend with you, the more they invest with you, and the more time you have to share your expertise, impress them and encourage them to connect with you. Forty-five minutes is the minimum. Ninety minutes is great. The more, the better.

- **What else is happening?** If something else is happening at this meeting, it might not be the right night for you to speak. You do not want anything that takes attention away from you and your talk.

Preparing Your Speech

After you are booked, you have to decide what to say and how you want to say it. Ask questions so you can customize your speech for that particular audience.

Your speech needs to deliver value to the audience. Fill it with benefits, tell stories, and give tips and advice. Weave in three compelling, memorable sound bites—short, catchy phrases that capture people's attention. Do not try to be funny. If you have humor in your talk, let it come naturally from the content. Mention a few facts and statistics and keep them to a minimum. Mention their sources to add credibility to what you are saying.

> *"Speak clearly, if you speak at all;*
> *carve every word before you let it fall."*
> —Oliver Wendell Holmes, American jurist

Prepare a handout that includes key points from your talk. Be sure to include your contact information on each page. Build in some audience participation activities, such as asking participants to write down three action steps they can take in the next couple of days. Your handout is a take-away that reminds people of the value you brought to the program.

Practice your talk so you can give it without notes. Do not memorize it! Memorizing makes you sound robotic and cold. Learn the points you want to make, the stories or client examples you want to share and the tips you want to be sure to include. Know them so well you can talk about them to a stranger in an elevator and sound perfectly natural. If you need prompts, prepare a one-page outline with key points and use your handout to stay on track.

By the way, never use a podium if you can avoid it. It puts a barrier between you and the audience and makes you less engaging. I always ask for a small, cocktail-size table near the area where I will speak. That is where I place my water and my outline, in case I need to look at it.

Deliver Value

If you feel nervous before speaking, go to the restroom and loosen up with some physical movements and mouth exercises. Raise your arms, pump them, smile, take deep breathes and *howl*. Calm your nerves with a pep talk and positive statements about giving a powerful speech that inspires people to take action and attracts valuable strategic alliance partners. Remind yourself that you are an expert and know your business!

Have fun and enjoy the speech. Make eye contact with different parts of the room, so everyone thinks you are talking just to him or her. Do not be one of those people who says they do not need a microphone—always take it. The microphone adds authority to your voice and helps with projection to keep the audience engaged.

Speak clearly and with confidence. Remember, you are the expert on your topic. The audience is there to hear what you have to say and to learn something new and exciting. Be enthusiastic and create verbal pictures. Tell compelling stories the audience can relate to and use examples from your business about how you solved problems and how they can too.

> *"Make sure you have finished speaking before your audience has finished listening."*
> —Dorothy Sarnoff, America entertainer and image consultant

Extend Yourself and Be Available at a Presentation

Always get to a presentation early so you can be 100 percent set up before the first attendee arrives. This way you are available to meet everyone and to mingle before your talk. Extend yourself and greet people. Remember you are not only there to give a speech, you are there to build your network. Find out who is in the room. Act like the host or hostess and extend yourself first to new people.

When I want to meet people, I walk up to them, extend my hand and say, "Hi, I haven't met you yet. I'm Caterina." This assertive introduction is always welcomed because people appreciate being approached in networking situations. It is an easy way to start a conversation. In addition, audience members will be more engaged and interested in your talk if they have met you one-on-one before your speech.

After Your Presentation—Follow Up Fast

The day after your speech, take any actions to which you committed. Within 24 hours, contact anyone who said they wanted to hear from you. For best results when leaving phone messages, stand, be positive and be enthusiastic. Keep your message short—it has been shown that the shorter a phone message is, the quicker it is returned.

Even though much of your audience will be impressed by you and leave feeling you are the expert, many will not be ready to be a client or see an immediate opportunity for referrals or strategic alliances.

That is fine. However, you lose all future opportunities if you do not stay in touch. That is why this next tip is crucial. During your speech, you want to tell the audience you will give them something for attending. This could be a free e-book, special report or audio download. This way you gather everyone's email address, allowing you to stay in touch.

After I meet individuals in person at a speech, I invite them to be my friend on Facebook®, ask them to connect with me on LinkedIn® and follow them on Twitter®. Time permitting, I include a personal note. This has resulted in many opportunities and new clients over the last few years. Through online social networking, you continue the relationships that started at the time of your presentation.

While this chapter has focused primarily on live and in-person speeches, I want you to know that teleclasses, webinars and radio interviews are equally valuable for building your network. For more on these other kinds of speeches, see *Using Virtual Events to Build Your Network* by Lynn Pearce on page 185, and Ana Lucia Novak's chapter, *Build Connections Quickly with Your Own Talk Radio Show* on page 197.

I have a goal to do eight to twelve marketing speeches, teleclasses, webinars and radio interviews every month. When I meet this goal, my network and revenue grow because of both the exposure and the new strategic alliance partners I meet and connect with along the way. These are usually the people hosting me as a featured speaker into the future..

I encourage you to set a goal in your business today for how often you want to speak to new people each month in order to grow your network, increase your visibility and get new clients.

Get busy. Pick your topic, find your audience, create your criteria and your speaker sheet and get yourself booked. By doing so consistently, you can ensure you have a thriving profitable and sustainable business.

CATERINA RANDO, MA, MCC
Business Strategist, Speaker, Publisher

Making your business thrive

(415) 668-4535
cat@caterinarando.com
www.caterinarando.com
www.caterinaspeaks.com
www.thrivebooks.com

Caterina Rando's mission is to show entrepreneurs how to build thriving businesses. She is a sought-after speaker, business strategist and author of the national bestseller, *Learn to Power Think,* from Chronicle Books. She is featured as a success expert in six other leading business books including *Build It Big, Get Clients Now, Get Slightly Famous* and *Incredible Business.*

Since 1993, Caterina has been providing consulting and training programs that ensure entrepreneurs succeed. Through her Business Breakthrough Summit, Sought-after-Speaker Summit and Social Media Marketing Summit for Women in Business, she and her team show entrepreneurs how to become recognized as experts, think and plan strategically and significantly grow their revenue.

Caterina is also the founder of THRIVE Publishing™, a company that publishes multi-author books, including this book, for experts who want to share their message with a greater market. Caterina holds a bachelor of science degree in organizational behavior and a master of arts degree in life transitions counseling psychology. She is a certified personal and professional coach (CPPC) and a master certified coach (MCC), the highest designation awarded by the International Coaching Federation.

More Make Your Connections Count

Now that you have learned many things about how to make your connections count, the next step is to take action. Get started applying what you have learned in the pages of this book.

We want you to know that we are here to help and inspire you meet your professional and personal objectives. The following pages list where we are geographically located. Regardless of where our companies are, many of us provide a variety of services over the phone or through webinars, and we welcome the opportunity to travel to your location or invite you to ours.

You can find out more about each of us by reading our bios at the end of our chapters, or by visiting our websites, listed below and on the following pages.

When you are ready for one-on-one consulting or group training from any of the co-authors in this book—we are available! When you call us, let us know you have read our book, and we will provide you with a free phone consultation to determine your needs and how to best serve you.

United States

Alabama
Bruce Bright, LtCol USMC (Ret) CCIM, CPC   www.ontargetleading.com

California
Joanne Lange   www.thepersonalassistant.com
Gail Nott   www.gailnott.com
Ana Lucia Novak   www.socialana.com
Lynn Pearce   www.virtualeventmaven.com
Caterina Rando, MA, MCC   www.caterinarando.com
                                www.caterinaspeaks.com
PJ Van Hulle   www.realprosperityinc.com

Connecticut
Anne Garland, ASID   www.annegarlandenterprises.com
Nannette Bosh, CPC   www.nannetteboshinc.com

Georgia
Lori Barber   www.elementsimage.com

Illinois
Sima Dahl, MBA   www.parlaycommunications.com

Maryland
Ken Rochon   www.perfectnetworker.com

Minnesota
Betty Liedtke, CDC   www.findyourburiedtreasure.com

Pennsylvania

Michelle R. Donovan   www.michellerdonovan.com

Cathy Jennings   www.nopressurenetworking.com

Texas

Patty Farmer   www.pattyfarmer.com

Utah

Jenny Bywater   www.thebooster.com

Canada

Ontario

Mirella Zanatta   www.firstimpressionsimageconsulting.com

Eleanor Parker, MBA   www.eleanorparkerandcompany.com

       www.sendoutcards.com/eleanorparker

Alberta

Sandra Fuentes   www.sandraspassion.com

SherryLynn Wrenn   www.sherspassion.com

THRIVE Publishing develops books for experts who want to share their knowledge with more and more people. We provide our co-authors with a proven system, professional guidance and support, producing quality, multi-author, how-to books that uplift and enhance the personal and professional lives of the people they serve.

We know that getting a book written and published is a huge undertaking. To make that process as easy as possible, we have an experienced team with the resources and know-how to put a quality, informative book in the hands of our co-authors quickly and affordably. Our co-authors are proud to be included in THRIVE Publishing books because these publications enhance their business missions, give them a professional outreach tool and enable them to communicate essential information to a wider audience.

You can find out more about our upcoming book projects at **www.thrivebooks.com**

Also from
THRIVE Publishing™

For more information
on this book, visit
www.executiveimagebook.com

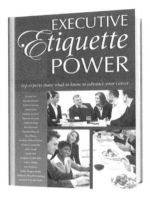

For more information
on this book, visit
www.execetiquette.com

For more information
on this book, visit
www.directsellingbook.com

For more information
on this book, visit
www.getorganizedtodaybook.com

Also from
THRIVE Publishing™

For more information
on this book, visit
www.incrediblebusinessbook.com

For more information
on this book, visit
www.mystylemywaybook.com

For more information
on this book, visit
www.momentrepreneurbook.com

For more information
on this book, visit
www.powerofcivilitybook.com

Become a Published Author with THRIVE Publishing

You may already be a match for one of our upcoming projects. Also, we are always looking for new ideas for multi-author books to publish, and we welcome yours.

One of our favorite kinds of projects is when we can partner with an organization or institution to publish a book that would be of particular interest to their members. In this case, sales of the book can be a revenue stream/fundraiser for the organization.

Last, and certainly not least, if you want to get going on your own book project, we can help.

Contact us to discuss any of the above options.

Phone: 415-668-4535
email: info@thrivebooks.com

For more copies of this book, *Make Your Connections Count*,
contact any of the co-authors or visit
www.connectionscountbook.com